Create Your Own Revolution

in helping repair our broken society

Mark Eyre is a self-employed personal development professional, helping people to achieve their potential in work and life. He previously worked for 25 years in a range of different organisations. Politically active during the 1980's and 1990's, he became disillusioned with how we are governed, and withdrew from active involvement. He is convinced that the time has come to put this right! This book sets out the steps we can all take to create a better society, and make ourselves feel better in the process.

Create Your Own Revolution

in helping repair our broken society

Mark Eyre

Arena Books

The right of Mark Eyre to be identified as author of this book
has been asserted in accordance with the Copyright, Designs and Patents Act 1988.

First published in 2016 by Arena Books

Arena Books
6 Southgate Green
Bury St. Edmunds
IP33 2BL

www.arenabooks.co.uk

Distributed in America by Ingram International, One Ingram Blvd., PO Box
3006, La Vergne, TN 37086-1985, USA.

Mark Eyre

Create Your Own Revolution *in helping repair our broken society*

British Library cataloguing in Publication Data. A catalogue record for this
book is available from the British Library.

ISBN-13   978-1-909421-66-0
BIC classifications:- VFJ, JFF, JFH, HP, JFM, JFS, VS, HPQ.

Printed and bound by Lightning Source UK

Cover design
by Jason Anscomb

Typeset in
Times New Roman

Create your own revolution

Introduction – In the beginning

- *If a man does not keep pace with his companions, perhaps it is because he hears a different drummer – **Henry David Thoreau***

I'm sitting down to write this book in the middle of what seems like a tumultuous time for the UK and the western world. The European elections concluded in May 2014, with anti-establishment and extremist parties gaining ground at the expense of those parties who have traditionally governed each country. The UK is currently 'considering her position' within the EU. Within the UK, the Scottish referendum campaign recently concluded with a narrow vote to continue the Union with the rest of the United Kingdom, though not on current terms and conditions. Nationalism has also been on the rise throughout the British Isles, primarily through the Scottish National Party and the UK Independence party. However, nationalist and regional demands are increasing in Wales and Cornwall, not to mention Northern Ireland. What I've talked about so far is just the politics.

Economically, there remains significant austerity and hardship following the banking collapse in autumn 2008, and the subsequent economic recession. There is anger at the size of bank bonuses, concern with immigration, and disillusion at the behaviour of big business, while at the same time we continue to move towards becoming a "global economy."

I used the word "tumultuous" at the start of this introduction. Yet there is a different side to all this. The aforementioned European elections saw parties winning throughout the British Isles with only 10% of the eligible adult population voting for them. Most voters were apparently unable to get up, leave their house and vote. Public campaigns to protest may be loud, but they usually fail, and mask a much greater number of us who appear not to care anymore. It's either that or we believe there's no point in even trying to change anything.

CREATE YOUR OWN REVOLUTION

Behind all this, day after day, and month after month, we are fed a diet of crisis ridden news that has the effect of encouraging apathy and resignation. The dominant game in our society encourages us to submit to rule by fear, to settle rather than aspire, and to turn a blind eye to injustice.

I want to encourage people to stop playing the game, do things differently, and stop buying what we get fed by our society. I refuse to believe that a society that is governed by fear is the best we can achieve, while hope and aspiration sit on the sidelines. But we are governed by a culture of fear – and that does not serve us well. We do not have epidemics of obesity, stress, depression and alcohol abuse in the western world because people feel good about themselves. We have these things because people don't feel good. It is time we did something about that.

I believe that it's time to stand up, and stop colluding in the game that's being driven by the System we live under. There have been many fine examples of how to do this down the years. It's time that we stood for some of these finest examples ourselves, rather than standing by. The likes of Martin Luther King, Mohandas Gandhi and Nelson Mandela, as well as being positive characters, were against injustice. They sought themselves to make changes to the System. They did not seek change by lowering themselves to the same level of the injustice that they fought against.

It is incumbent on those of us who think differently to start beating the drum in a different way, and encourage other people to wake up.

People lead stressful lives as it is without needing more stress. Work is long hours, often invading our private lives as smart phones and tablet computers 'liberate' us. The result is that we are left with no time to think. The best thing we can do when at home is switch on the TV set, and watch soap operas, virtual reality TV, or the 24-hour news. In so doing, we ignore the soap opera and virtual reality dimension of the society we live in! We are living a soap operatic virtual reality existence right now, in a play with a script that drives us to behave in certain ways, and fulfil certain roles. Oh yes, many of us are acting just as much (and maybe as badly) as in those plots we see on TV.

This book represents a different way to be. It is not so much about what we want - it's about who we are, and how we want to be in our lives. We can choose to go along with the play, as most people do. The majority tend to end up simply complying with authority. But even the rebels are playing the game. As we shall see, our society needs rebels to keep going. That's why most attempts to change things don't work, or at least not much changes as a result. Even those who opt out and don't vote are going along with the game – no one has declared the European elections to be invalid because only a third of the population voted. Shareholders also opt out and don't turn up to Company shareholder meetings, and so on.

Yet, if we are honest with ourselves, most of us know things are wrong in the society we live in. Put a group of people in a room to discuss how things are, and there is likely to be a significant consensus emerging. There is general consternation at the gap between rich and poor being so wide, while banks pay bonuses despite not serving small businesses and society well. There is despair at how a supposedly affluent society can have so many desperately poor and homeless people living in its midst, and that this is tolerated. There is anger about utility companies taking liberties with customers, raising prices despite making record profits for their shareholders – oh, and record salaries for directors. There is concern about levels of immigration and impact on local culture, some of it racist, but much of it not, and borne of fear.

The one common factor behind all of this is the sense that the authorities, those in power, are not listening to us, and maybe do not even care. The public response is to list the people to blame, and make scapegoats of them – bankers, politicians, bureaucrats, do gooders, other nations, you name them. The blame game plays into the System's hands, as essentially it is a form of futile rebellion. The question is, do we want to blame others for society's ills, or do we want to do something about it? I'm writing this book for those of you who want to do the latter.

We already know what needs to be fixed. We just need the courage to take a step back and start fixing it, rather than waiting for someone else to do it.

Why do we connive in society's game?

Most of us connive because we are conditioned by our upbringing, education and early experiences of work to adapt to the point that we stop agitating for what we believe in. Gradually we learn to "play the game." The trouble with this approach is that playing the game simply prolongs the game.

We see the results in the cynicism that is all around us. We see big companies now, for example, touting the fact that they pay their taxes as a unique selling point – how virtuous are we for paying our taxes? How cynical a ploy is that? Surely, businesses should be paying their taxes, full stop? Can you imagine going to a job interview, being asked why you should get the job, and saying "because I'm honest, for example I pay my taxes on time." If you said that, you'd be laughed out of the interview with no job in sight! Yet this is exactly what companies now market themselves as doing, and they get lauded for it. We should not be surprised by this when - as we shall see - corporations are currently more important than people are.

This book is not a quick fix. It won't result in everything changing tomorrow. Contrary to what we see everywhere around us, quick fixes simply do not work, though we might like the idea. What this book can spark is a genuine, long-term fix, by changing the game forever. Furthermore, we won't just end up fixing our broken society, we will fix ourselves to boot, and become better human beings in the process. Our society will inevitably be transformed if enough of us start playing a different game – perhaps as little as 5-10% of the population following the approaches outlined in this book, would lead to major change in society. It would be enough to start a transformational movement.

The irony in all this is that most people behave as if nothing can be done about any of this. Yet there has never been a greater opportunity to ignite change for the better. We could choose to do things differently. Social media and the internet give us all a bigger platform to communicate with other people, and publicise our thoughts and actions. How many trends these last few years were started online, and spread beyond that? Those seeking changes of Government in Egypt, for example, used Facebook to help their cause. Rioters in Britain in recent years have used social media to communicate, and even to post videos that subsequently were publicised on TV. It is ironic that rioters and terrorists know better how to use social media nowadays to get things to happen than the rest of us do. It's about time that changed.

How can we make the change happen?

As we will see, the key to transforming society is to begin the process of transforming ourselves. The good news is that all we need to do to change things is to rediscover talents that we were all born with, but have since been educated out of using, as we 'mature.' They are talents that will turn us from rationalising and being small, to thinking and being big. They are talents that give us the spark to live, hope for the future, and determination to see things through. They are all talents that the average 2-3 year old child has in spades! As we will see, bringing a bit more of the child out in us will lead to significant change on its own.

So, if you're sick and tired of feeling sick and tired, you can change how things are, if you stop conniving in the system and play a different game instead. This doesn't mean disengaging from society completely. It does mean taking a step back and looking at what's happening. It means becoming less consumed in what is going on. Society is a drama, and it will try to suck us into the game, but we can choose to transcend it once we realise what is going on.

Transforming society or self-help?

As a young man, I studied Economics and Politics at University. As a middle-aged man, I have worked extensively in the field of personal and professional development. So I've read books down the years about politics and society, and I've also read plenty of books about self-help.

In all that time, one thought has always struck me, and it is this. When I read or hear about politics and society, I have often heard passion about society, and what needs to change. Yet there is little about how we develop as human beings to achieve our own potential. Even the influential political writers of the past, from Karl Marx to Milton Friedman had nothing to say on personal development. How self-aware are most modern politicians of how they come across? Has David Cameron or Alex Salmond ever done anything to better themselves from a personal development viewpoint? What about George Bush or Barack Obama? Listen to any political debate, and you have to conclude that the answer is a resounding 'no'. We listen to political leaders who largely behave like stroppy children.

It's almost as if politicians go into politics to avoid talking about how they might improve themselves. Redeeming society becomes their means of escaping their own demons, of avoiding the need to confront their own character.

Meanwhile, walk into any bookshop or look online, and you find a mountain of books from personal development authors. They give advice on everything from feeling more confident to losing weight, achieving all you want, to being more self-aware. They offer you the opportunity to transform yourself. These self-help gurus submerge themselves in this material while meticulously avoiding dealing with any wider topics of society. They have such strong feelings and views on how we can improve ourselves as individuals, but no view whatsoever on how we might improve ourselves collectively. Doesn't that strike you as a bit odd? The salvation of self means little unless it comes with the salvation of society.

I believe it is possible to have the best of both worlds. We can work on improving the way our society works, changing its values and priorities while at the same time improving our own position. The key, as we shall see, is to find the core of our own humanity again, and with it our potential to develop as human beings. By contrast, focusing on either self-betterment, or bettering society without looking at ourselves, is going to generate little improvement. That's why so few politicians make any positive impact, and so few self-help books achieve genuine impact on individuals who read them. That's why transformational, long lasting change remains elusive.

Why I'm writing this book

For more years than I care to remember, I have been disillusioned with the society I live in. It has simply felt wrong. Spending much of my life working for Corporations that were fundamentally undemocratic felt wrong to me. The futility of voting in elections that changed nothing of significance also felt wrong. From my early adult days of being politically active, I became gradually more cynical (though I've denied being a cynic on many occasions!) I wandered around, like a Corporate Hippie, looking for something better, and generally failing to find it. I changed political party, but that didn't work, so I drifted away. I changed jobs, but that didn't work either, so I drifted on that one too!

I found some salvation by getting into self-employment, my own version of declaring independence. Now that helped, but I still had to get business from somewhere, to make a living. Being a self-employed personal development consultant enabled me to help other people live better work and home lives, by developing their potential as human beings. Now this was better, but it was not enough. I was left with a conundrum; how to encourage other people to believe in themselves and their potential, and empower themselves, when they live in a society that is manifestly unfair in how it works, sapping people's energy and will to live.

CREATE YOUR OWN REVOLUTION

This book is a response to that conundrum. What is more, the irony of ironies is that the key to transforming society is rooted in our own personal development as human beings, allied to understanding that we are all connected and have the power to change things.

I'm writing this book because I've met too many people who feel disillusioned, disenfranchised and helpless about what goes on around them. As a professional coach, I help people to pull their lives together, both in work and at times their outside life. There's nothing better than helping someone to turn their life around, become more confident, with more belief in their own abilities. That's great. However, the problem is that so many of the issues people face are the consequence of the society we live in, and how it is run. It is set up to produce people who lack confidence, are all too aware of their own limitations, and don't believe they can do anything, be anything or change anything.

I do not believe this to be true about anyone. We are all unique, talented people. We just need to believe this. Our society squanders human talent in the same way it squanders all other natural resources. Like so much in our garbage driven society, human beings are used, discarded and thrown away. It's no wonder so many of us feel bad!

Yet, deep down, when I talk to people who are in this place, they want something better. In my experience, most people are fundamentally decent and well intentioned. But these qualities are largely ignored or misdirected in the game we are sucked into playing. So I write as someone who has talked to thousands of people down the years, and who has drawn some conclusions from this.

I am not writing this book as an expert who believes he has all the answers. I am not. The answers will ultimately come from within all of us who engage with the issues I highlight. It follows that some areas of the book might be weaker than other parts. If I work on this, I might make some further improvements to it, I don't deny that. However, I'm not writing this to 'give all the solutions.' I'm writing it to encourage, and perhaps even to provoke, a dialogue because a dialogue between people is precisely what we need right now. Besides, after eight years of austerity and hardship, it's surely time to act. I am putting my views and thoughts up for debate, with the intention of sparking action for change. One theme I will talk about is the importance of taking action, and not just talking about it.

CREATE YOUR OWN REVOLUTION

I don't know whether this book will find a publisher, or whether I will end up giving it away for free. In many ways, I don't care. I passionately believe that society's game sells us short, and I want it to change – and for each of us to change ourselves, what we do and how we are. I'm writing this book because I want to get the message out to as many people as possible, and I will do whatever I can to achieve this.

I've lived my life long enough to realise that, out of disillusionment can come great clarity of thinking. Out of despair can bring hope for the future. Out of problems, opportunities can arise. So if you're ready to come out and play, let the games begin!

Mark Eyre
AKA the Corporate Hippie

Part 1 – The problem with society

Chapter 1 - What we all know

- *A 'no' uttered from deepest conviction is better and greater than a yes merely uttered to please, or what is worse, to avoid trouble –* **Mohandas Gandhi**

The Crisis

The society we live in is sick. We all know that, if we're honest with ourselves. From our politics to big business to large organisations so influential in our society, we live in the midst of a crisis. It is a crisis of confidence, beliefs, values and behaviour. What's more it is a continual crisis; it is not going away anytime soon.

We see this crisis manifested in the behaviour of politicians, with expenses scandals and mistrust of motives at a record high, while electoral participation is at a record low. In the USA we saw the near breakdown of the federal government, as funds ran out due to a dispute between the American Congress and President Obama. Anti-establishment and extremist parties are gaining in popularity on both sides of the Atlantic.

We see it in the behaviour of big business, and more than anywhere else in the behaviour of our financial institutions. Banks made bad investments in the interests of huge bonuses, and the public are left to pick up the bill for it. We have paid for this folly with higher taxes, and in many cases with our jobs, while those very same banks aren't slow to condemn their customers who fail to pay their debts on time. We see it in utility companies treating customers with disdain, and many organisations now make it almost impossible for people to contact them directly. If you try to phone to complain about some aspect of service, you invariably get transferred to a call centre – possibly abroad. You get passed around, after pressing one of five numbers, depending on what your call is about. Then if you phone again, you almost certainly have to speak to a different person, and relay your whole story all over again. These companies don't have time to ring you back and help you with your problems, but they have plenty of time to bombard you with new and exciting offers and services.

We see this crisis in our airports, where checking in feels more like entering a prison than anything else. You now have to remove half your clothes to go through the security gates. We see it in education, where the only thing that matters is giving pupils enough knowledge to get a job. Any other knowledge is often viewed as extravagant. We see it in a property market in which houses are seen as an investment, rather than a place where people live. The result of which is that, if you live in London, you have no chance of buying your own property unless you inherit one, or inherit money.

We see it in health, where epidemic levels of stress reign, along with other recent illness epidemics like obesity and depression. Since 2011, stress has been the number one reason given for sick absence at work. We see it on our streets with homeless people, and the number of food banks that now exist in what is supposed to be a wealthy country. Shame on us all.

We see it not just in Scotland and the UK, but in every country in the western world. In Greece, Portugal, Spain and Ireland, we have seen savage cutbacks that make those in the UK seem mild by comparison. In Europe, including the UK, we see the rise of nationalism and in some cases repression. We see it in the number of wars we have fought to fight terror, while at the same time killing hundreds of thousands of people in the name of supposedly civilised values.

We see it in young people, who have a more exciting time playing virtual reality computer games than they have in real life. The excitement, risk-taking and self-betterment are confined to a fantasy game that changes nothing in real life. Escapism has become the new reality for teenagers, just as reality TV has done the same for the rest of us. We substitute fantasy for real life, because real life sucks.

It is quite clear that the wrong things are prioritised and valued by our existing social order. What's more, most people when they talk about what they really think will recognise this. They will see a shameful list of things that are wrong with the way things are. Here are ten things about our existing society that should put us all to shame, if we think about it. I have listed them in no particular order.

CREATE YOUR OWN REVOLUTION

1. **The demise of the elderly** – In most ancient societies, age is venerated. Older people were listened to, as they had been through life, and learned their lessons. If the young had any sense, they would listen and learn. Nowadays, older people are more often thrown onto the scrapheap. Once you've reached fifty, you're often considered to be over the hill. Older employees are often the first to go when redundancies strike. The dominant culture in our society diminishes our reputation for being energetic, dynamic and ambitious, as we become older. Once you've retired from work, many in society will see you as good for not much more than looking after grandchildren. Many pensioners are discarded as being useful to society in the same way that rubbish is discarded. It's not true that all people think this way, but our society behaves increasingly as if this is true.

2. **The decline of pensions** - This is another reflection on how the elderly are seen. However, it is more than that. It is the way in which the pensions of millions of people have been rendered increasingly worthless as the years progress. As pension funds have grown huge funding deficits, employee contributions have risen significantly while the promised benefits have diminished. There are many reasons for this, including poor returns, bad investment decisions, and people retiring earlier and living longer over the past 25 years. However, another reason for this is that when investment returns were good in the 1980's and early 1990's, many companies stopped paying their pension contributions. This was euphemistically referred to as "taking a contribution holiday." However, against this background of declining pensions for most of us, Executive pensions have survived largely intact. So have the pensions of the political classes. Those in power have looked after themselves, while the rest of us have been left to fend for ourselves.

3. **Food banks and executive pay** - In a supposedly civilised, affluent society, we have growing numbers of food banks. These highlight one end of the income scale, while at the other end top salaries and other wealth indicators continue to rise. Being poor and in need of food is not a lifestyle choice. It is a consequence of the way our society runs.

   In 2013-14, more than 900,000 people in the UK received emergency food from food banks, compared to fewer than 350,000 in 2012-13, according to the Trussell Trust. This is happening in an allegedly well-off society that is supposed to be experiencing economic growth after the long recession from 2008-12. Rising costs of living combined with stagnant wages are "causing more people to live on a financial knife edge where any change in circumstances can plunge them into poverty." (1). If this were not enough, on 16th June 2014, the High Pay Centre commented on OECD figures that show that "the poorest fifth of the UK population are the poorest in Western Europe." (2)

In contrast, we have seen an explosion in Executive pay in the UK. The *Guardian* newspaper highlighted on 22nd November 2011 that the High Pay Commission had reported on "the 30-year trend of increasing top pay that has left the earnings gap between the very richest and the rest of society wider than at any point since Queen Victoria was on the throne." (3) In 2010-11, executive pay in FTSE100 companies grew by 49%. This is a scandalous contrast to how the very poorest are treated.

Another source on this subject is the High Pay Centre. It reported in 2014 that top bosses in FTSE 100 companies now earn up to 143 times more than their average employee does, compared to a figure of 47 times in 1998. Deborah Hargreaves, Director at the High Pay Centre, commented on this increasing disparity between top executive pay and average employee pay as follows:

"Britain's executives haven't got so much better over the past two decades. The only reason why their pay has increased so rapidly compared to their employees is that they are able to get away with it." (4)

Does that clear things up? We should be ashamed of this.

4. **The accumulation of debt** - The global economy runs on the basis of debt, and the UK reflects this trend with interest (sorry about the pun!) Never in history have so many people been in debt up to, and beyond, their eyeballs. Britain is proud to call itself a "property-owning democracy." Yet the reality is that the banks own the vast majority of homes, with the rest of us owing the banks. Meanwhile, credit card debts are at record levels, and students routinely leave higher education owing many thousands of pounds - the sort of debt you used to have when you took out a mortgage. It's no wonder that the biggest fear many people have is the fear of running out of money.

In April 2014, research from the Institute of Fiscal Studies (IFS) stated that, with rising University tuition fees, the average graduate would pay around £66,897 to repay their student loans. (5) Given the average UK graduate starting salary in 2014 is £21,000, it might take quite a long time for this amount to be paid off. As a result, 75% of graduates are likely to reach their 50's by the time they manage to clear this debt, if they manage to clear it at all. It's no wonder why so many people see the purpose of education as simply to get people a job.

You might think that as long as you find and hold down work, you would successfully pay your debts off, or at least not see them rise any further. But that is sadly a mistaken assumption. The BBC's Panorama programme reported on 6th October 2014 on how even two-parent working families were struggling to survive at a time when the Government are cutting welfare and tax credits for these same groups. Among many examples was a couple, both working for Tesco, who were still living below the poverty line. This gives the lie to the claim that you can work yourself out of poverty, and is scandalous.

5. **The rise of image** - Image has become everything in our society. Image matters, from the way you look and dress, to the self-portrait you put on Facebook for others to see, to corporate image. Makeovers and branding have become the twin engines of image. Manufactured boy and girl bands have replaced musicians, with how they look being of more importance than how talented they are. Image fixation makes fashions all-important, which matters to our capitalist system because it means businesses can sell us more over time, as we try to keep up with everyone else.

The obsession with image is one driver that fuels the epidemic of diet disorders among teenagers and young adults, particularly women, who are encouraged to attain a particular body shape if they are to be considered 'attractive.'

6. **People as consumers, full stop** - People are no longer people, or at least that's not what matters most. Instead, we are consumers, who gobble things up, and then need new things to gobble afterwards. New gadgets, clothes, more exotic holidays, bigger houses and new cars are all wanted as we attempt to chase nirvana. Of course, we never make it to that destination. There is always something else that we need first. Fuelling consumerism is the fact that most things are disposable

nowadays, and will soon need replacing. From computers to cars, fairly regular replacement is required, perhaps every 3-4 years for a computer or laptop. Replacement is the fuel that feeds the capitalist monster. The pursuit of the quick fix also feeds the monster, as they often prove to be temporary fixes or not a fix at all.

7. **Invasion and war** - Let's face it, how many wars have we had in the last ten to fifteen years? We've had the War on Terror, with hundreds of thousands of Iraqis and Afghanis dying in the name of western civilisation. Does anyone spot the contradiction in this? Of course, it does not have to be an actual war. Our society is very good at focusing on all sorts of wars. We've had war in hospitals, schools, high street wars, and even a war on litter, as we seek things to literally and metaphorically fight against. Are we incapable of finding a more productive approach to life?

Taking the case of the invasion of Iraq in 2003, the New Scientist quoted a UK study that reported that the invasion could be directly attributed for the deaths of some 655,000 Iraqis. This represents some 2.5% of the population of Iraq. An equivalent number of British dead would be 1 ½ million. Meanwhile, we are now 100 years on from the outbreak of World War One, when around 700,000 British soldiers died (6). Even 100 years on, many of us feel the pain of what that war did to our nation. So just how can destroying the lives of Iraqis, most of them totally innocent of any wrongdoing, advance the cause of civilisation? What war on terror were we stopping by doing this? We cannot be surprised when the whole Middle East is sliding into chaos and anarchy fuelled by hatred and self-righteousness.

8. **Modern illnesses** - Since 2011, stress has been the single biggest certifiable illness preventing people from attending work. Depression is at record levels, and a walk through any shopping centre or mall will highlight the other modern phenomenon - the epidemic of obesity that we now face. At the other end of the scale, eating disorders and bulimia are also rife, fuelled partly by the importance of image spoken about earlier. These modern illnesses are placing increasing strain on the health services throughout the western world, particularly in the UK and USA.

9. **The rise of nationalism** - With competition being the fuel of capitalism, and war the buzz word in society, the power of dividing

people into "us" and "them" is pervasive. It is therefore no surprise to see the rise of nationalism taking hold in the west. From Russia and the Ukraine to Scotland's independence movement, British anti-European sentiment and other European separatist groups in Spain and Belgium, nationalist (as opposed to patriotic) sentiment is taking hold. In addition to being short-sighted, petty and divisive, nationalism in Europe usually means bad news, as any historian will tell you. As we commemorate the 100th anniversary of the outbreak of World War One, this reason for shame should give us all pause for reflection. In Europe, nationalist sentiment expressed anywhere other than sports arenas, or perhaps in appreciation of culture and history, is invariably bad news.

10. **Money is king** - "People are our most important asset" is the mantra trotted out by Executives in corporations and politicians in countries. It might be what most people want to hear, but it simply is not true. Carry out an armed robbery (a crime against money) and you will receive a heavier prison sentence than you would for manslaughter, attempted murder or rape. Banks get bailed out while people are allowed to go bankrupt by the same banks. Even whole countries full of people are forced to repay debts to the very banks who went bust in the first place, creating the financial crisis. People are evicted from their homes so more profitable activities can be substituted on the land.

Developing the last theme a bit further, consider the professions and who gets rewarded. Professions who serve people are highly regarded by public opinion, but don't get all that well rewarded for what they do. Just think of teachers and nurses, for example - and you need a University degree to get into one of those professions nowadays. Now consider professions who primarily work with finances and money. Professions like banking, the stock market, and sales. Who receives the greater level of reward? There's no prize for getting the answer to that question correct!

The futility of change

Cynicism is rife in 2015. In many ways, it is justified, as it seems that there's little chance of things changing for the better. The system that governs our lives continues to suck us into its game, and despite how we feel, we continue to participate. There is no better example of the apparent futility of change than the Presidency of Barack Obama. Obama comes across to me as a man of principle, and with strongly held beliefs about how things could be. He was elected on a promise of change, with the slogan "yes we can" being a key factor behind his first election victory. Four years later, he won for a second time.

So what happened? Apart from some long overdue healthcare reforms, very little has changed. The American interrogation camp at Guantanamo, which Obama originally campaigned against, is still open in Cuba. US troops are still fighting the war on terror begun by George Bush more than a decade earlier. There has been no significant social progress in the USA since 2008. On the face of it, the achievement has been modest at best.

Was Mr Obama lying when he spoke of his passion for change? Is he simply inept, and incapable of getting his way? I somehow doubt it. But I think this failure illustrates a key point - you cannot change the System by playing the System game. The System will always win in the end, as it has in Mr Obama's case. Of course, the System game in the USA includes the "balance of powers" where the Houses of Congress and the US Supreme Court remain independent of the President. When the original US constitution was established, the balance of power was seen as a key guarantor of liberty and a protection against tyranny. What it has become in modern American society is a guarantee that nothing will ever change.

If you consider this view to be a little cynical, let's look at the UK instead. In the last seventy years, two major political breakthroughs have been achieved, using different strategies - and both ultimately failed to change fundamentally how our society operates. Both involved trying to beat the System at its own game, and both failed because beating the System at its own game is well nigh impossible. In 1945, after World War Two, the UK Labour Party achieved a historical breakthrough with a manifesto for radical change. They swept to power with a record majority after performing only modestly well in previous elections. They planned to create a National Health Service (NHS), nationalise whole sections of industry, and create the visionary socialist society so many had talked about for so long.

The 1945 Labour Government is the nearest Britain came to a major change in society. However, within a few years, this Government many of whose supporters had never expected to win began to run out of ideas. The dominant orthodoxy adapted to their radical agenda, and even the Conservatives accepted the NHS and nationalised industries. Within six years, Labour had lost power, and within fifteen years it was hard to tell the main parties apart. The case for radical change was gradually whittled away, with the NHS being the only institution that has survived.

The second breakthrough in the UK was not sudden, but gradual. In the 1960's, fuelled by increasing discontent at the two main political parties, the Liberals began to attract a protest vote, and gradually increased support at general and local elections. After years of coming close, as the Alliance in the 1980's and the formation of the Liberal Democrats, the party finally made a breakthrough in 2010. The first thing that happened was that they did a deal with the Conservatives to form a coalition government. Yet most Liberal voters would not have supported the Conservatives, as most considered themselves to be on the side of change. Paradoxically, the closer the Liberals came to power, the less distinguishable they seemed from the old parties they claimed to be so different from.

In short then, the system undermined and assimilated the Labour party when they made a sudden breakthrough in 1945. It also assimilated the Liberals before they'd even made their breakthrough in 2010. The lesson I draw from this is stark and clear. You cannot significantly change the System by either sudden break-through or gradual build up. Concerted attempts to change things fail. The System, and its actors, will act to preserve itself.

That leaves, to my mind, only two options – overthrow of the System, or learning to play a different game entirely. Most of us would not support the first option, and not just because "we're British." Most evidence is that overthrowing the System generally doesn't work. We will go on to look at why this is later in the book.

For the moment, we need to understand better what this all-powerful System is we are living under. So we're going to look at its characteristics in a bit more detail, before we move onto how we deal with it, and play a different game. Exposing the System's Big Society game is a significant first step.

Chapter 2 - The 'Big Society' game

- *Society attacks early when the individual is helpless - **B F Skinner***

The art of sleepwalking

Have any of you watched the film called *The Matrix*? In case you haven't, it is a film that depicts how the world has been taken over by a robotic race that was originally created by humans. They have enslaved the human race so they can live off our energy. In reality, we human beings are literally born artificially, and raised in captivity housed in incubators, until we cease to be useful.

Of course, we would never accept this fate, would we? So, in the Matrix, the master race induces us into an elaborate dream, where we believe we are alive and living in the western world. That way, we believe we are living, and so don't resist our captivity. This virtual society is called the matrix, and we are all made part of it.

Now, in the film version, enough people realise that it's all an elaborate hoax, wake up to reality as it really is, and begin to fight back. But then of course in films, the heroes generally win. It would be funny if it wasn't such an accurate portrayal of what goes on in this life we are living.

Are you insane Mark, I hear you ask? Before you answer your own question, let's consider the parallels. Granted, there isn't a master race as such. But our society does work according to a set of rules, like a matrix. Most people live day to day lives blithely ignorant of this, just accepting or at least going along with what we're told to do, or not do. A few people wake up to this, a waking up often sparked by the sense that "things aren't right" in some way. A few openly rebel against the dominant System orthodoxy, but are then persecuted as the enemy, with most of the population either indifferent to what's going on, or even complying with the persecution.

It doesn't look so different now, does it?

So why don't more people wake up to this situation? Part of the reason lies in our increasing preoccupation with trivia, largely thanks to the antics of the media and entertainment industry. Over the last 25 years in particular (with warning signs before this that reach back to the 1950's), we have seen the erection of frivolity – and I use these words deliberately! Turn the TV on any evening nowadays, and what do we find on the main channels? We see increasingly unrealistic soap operas with plot lines that would never happen in our lives. We see reality TV that covers everything except reality. What is real about the British TV programme *Big Brother*? We have the development of increasingly sophisticated computer and TV games that invite us to live much of our leisure life playing them. Some teenagers now live more for their virtual life, than they do for their real one.

We spend more time posting messages on Facebook and Twitter than we do talking to the people who are in the same room as we are. We have the placebo of celebrity, the evolution of people who are famous for simply being famous. There was a day when you actually had to achieve something to become famous. That is not the case anymore. I'm not going to name names, but we all know who they are. Wives of footballers are high up on this list!

We are deflected from what's really going on by the epidemic of triviality, frivolity, celebrity and so called reality. In this fantasy world, what's really going on with us and our society doesn't matter. Even desperately poor people who starve are now put on TV for our entertainment. Isn't that a disgrace, if we stop to think about it? The trouble is most people don't stop to think.

But then, we have a law against stopping, with a fifth word that ends in 'ity'. That word is 'activity'. We fill our lives with so much activity, and are encouraged to do this. We end up being so active that there is no time to think.

Those of you who remember reading George Orwell and Aldous Huxley at school might be struck by the irony of it all. In his most famous book, 1984, (1) Orwell painted a picture of a society driven by fear, which induced a desire among the population not to be noticed, because being noticed meant being singled out. That meant likely torture and death. The nation was always fighting a war, which kept the population absorbed so much that they didn't notice the declining living standards they had to deal with in their daily lives. The catch-all phrase that captured the paranoia in society was "big brother is watching you." Orwell would have appreciated the irony of a popular virtual TV programme being named after this phrase. The TV programme is an example of the deflection that takes attention away from all that is wrong in our society.

Orwell also described the concept of 'double-think', where we say one thing when we really mean another. For example, the Ministry of Truth existed to tell lies and propaganda, while the Ministry of Peace existed to make war. Nowadays, we are familiar with the idea of politics and big business being dominated by spin and PR. Governments now employ marketing and PR executives as spin doctors to get the 'right' message out to an increasingly cynical public. The public's reaction for the most part is to say 'fuck it' to politics, with increasing numbers of people no longer bothering to vote in elections.

Aldous Huxley meanwhile, in *Brave New World* (2) wrote of a society in which mindless entertainment and casual relationships were encouraged to take people's minds off the deeper question of why society was the way it was. Again, it sums up at least some of what has actually happened since.

We live in an era where charity giving, environmental awareness and even paying taxes have become areas in which businesses market themselves and their virtue. Most large businesses routinely employ people to manage donations to charity, or to coordinate their workforce to donate more to charity. Even worthwhile causes like 'Children in need' and 'Comic relief' allow businesses to spend a day showing how aware they are of wider community and global issues. But when the day is over, awareness drops again to its previous low level.

One global financial services company markets its social responsibility by pointing out how much tax it contributes to the countries it operates in. Now I could point out that the same Company also operated from a high number of offshore sites, which of course are designed not to pay tax. However, it shows how far we've come when simply paying tax is seen as some sort of virtue. It's like me claiming to be an ethical guy and the proof of this is that I paid so much tax last year. How does that prove my ethics?

Everything nowadays is a brand. Have you noticed how we are encouraged to find and define our own 'personal brand?' This is particularly so when we are job-seeking. What are your Unique Selling Points or USPs? Why would people want to buy you? Doesn't it strike you as strange how, rather than encouraging Companies to become more human, we are encouraging people to behave more like Companies? What's that all about?

We live in an era where all the propaganda is about global competition and choice. We are in competition with every other country on the planet, and we'd better become more efficient otherwise no one will bother to invest in us. But the benefits are all around us. After all, we can choose from among thousands of different makes of mobile phone. We can have any colour we want.

The let-down

The let-downs are many from the system we currently live in. Here are just a few.

The environment

We see politicians, business and the media trumpeting their green credentials. However, behind all this noise, our existing economic system is destroying the environment in which we live – and possibly the world. In 2012–13 for example, much of the south of England was badly flooded. Whether climate change is part of the reason, there is no doubt that another part of the reason was the decision taken by planning authorities to allow new houses to be built on flood plains. This inevitably made flooding more likely in two ways. First, by placing houses precisely in places that are vulnerable to flooding. Secondly, by reducing the capacity of surrounding areas to absorb excess water, leaving it with nowhere to go other than to flood places.

Consider too that the British Government, right now, is considering making it easier for fracking to take place under people's homes. At present, homeowners could challenge this in the Courts using the trespass laws, but a change in the law would affect this. So much for owning the ground our houses stand on! Now, there may be a case for hydraulic fracturing to get at shale gas, as a potential source of energy. However, the way the Government are proceeding suggests they aren't interested in addressing the disquiet many people feel about the environmental consequences of fracking for fuel.

An epidemic of debt

In recent years, we hear TV news commentators and even politicians bemoaning the lack of savings and levels of debt in our society. Yet our existing System can only survive on the basis of more and more people running up more and more debt. Go back to the 1950's and most people had no debt. That is not the case nowadays, with the vast majority of households running in the red. Everything from record mortgage level to massive credit card debts, to graduates nowadays having large debts before they even secure their first job. I saw a figure recently that suggested the average graduate in England graduates with some £44k worth of debt. (3)

If you doubt this, just check your own balance of assets and liabilities. Most of us will find out we're in the red.

Of course, this epidemic of debt puts us in debt literally to the System.

Lack of meaningful choice

The concept of choice is largely a myth. We see this all over the place. On the one hand, on some things, we have a huge range of choices on relatively trivial matters. From thousands of mobile phones to masses of different insurance policies and savings accounts, confectionary and cereals to name a few. Does it really matter which one we pick compared to another? I know some readers will have their favourite chocolate bar, but even if you do, it is not life changing. We have choices on who wins each televised talent competition or virtual TV show, but again this is hardly choice about a significant matter.

Contrast this with the potentially big decisions we have, like who runs the Government. I don't know about you, but increasingly elections feel to me like we're choosing between management committees to run the country. It's a choice between equally suited, equally booted politicians, who all say largely the same things and all believe largely the same things. So what's the point of voting at all? It's little wonder that such a small proportion of the electorate bother to vote consistently at all. Increasingly, it feels like voting doesn't make a difference. It's no wonder when political parties are funded from similar sources (like businesses and wealthy benefactors.) For many in our society, there is no meaningful choice when it comes to health and schools, life changing areas of our lives.

Behind the propaganda, the choice doesn't exist. Ask any parent who failed to get their child into the School they wanted. Ask any patient who has to wait to go into hospital for essential treatment. Even the thousands of mobile phones boil down to about half-a-dozen manufacturers.

CREATE YOUR OWN REVOLUTION

Self betterment

Human beings are born with the potential to better themselves, and children display this desire in abundance. They want to know why everything happens, try out different things to see what works, and to stretch their talent to see just what they can do. Contrast this to what happens as we get older. The System that is our society contains a lack of opportunity for self-betterment. The desire to better yourself is seen largely as a luxury, as conforming to the needs of society is given priority. Even the primary vehicle for self-betterment, education, is increasingly viewed as little more than a means to get us a job. Wider considerations are largely given lip service to the great God work. Don't just take my word for it. Take the views of distinguished educationalist Sir Ken Robinson. His widely popular presentation to a TED Conference in 2006, titled 'do schools kill creativity' laid the workings of our education system bare. He spoke of creative children being educated to believe they are not talented. Any child not conforming to a fairly narrow stereotype of what a child should be like is treated as in some way abnormal. It would be funny if it wasn't so sad. (4)

However, if school is a challenge, the workplace is far worse on this. Self betterment is largely confined to what will make you 'better' in some way at work, or make you more promotable. Anything else is seen as trivial, and given no priority. In this way, skills and talents that could be hugely useful to society are ignored or discarded.

Yet another irony is that as society has grown wealthier, self-improvement has been given lower and lower priority. Society's need for self-betterment does not exist in comparison to its need for us to simply produce and consume. Various studies, starting with the American psychologist Abraham Maslow, have suggested that people who pursue self-betterment comprise only 1-2 % of the population. (5) That would explain why self-help books are outsold by fiction novels. However, there is evidence that the desire for self-betterment is greater than 1%, but is suppressed in the vast majority of people. That's why so many people go through mid-life crises, which for many in the modern era begins much earlier than the forty-something that it used to.

It's ironic considering the advertising propaganda that you can have whatever you want, that the core principle of self-betterment is almost totally ignored. The principle that you can be whatever you want.

Declining incomes

Many of us have become used to the idea of declining living standards over the past few years, ever since the credit crunch and banking collapse. Propaganda tells us that at least we had rising living standards until that point, with the odd hiccough in between. We are raised to believe that the free market we live in has delivered prosperity and rising living standards.

Would it be a surprise to you if I challenge this bland assertion as fundamentally wrong? There is considerable evidence that, in the United States for example, real incomes have been in decline since 1970. Yes, since 1970! It seems scarcely credible that this could happen and no one noticed it. But it has happened, and many people have not noticed. Let me explain why this is.

First, incomes have gone up, but so have prices. More significantly, the working week has gone up too. Many employers now operate with the expectation that employees will put in extra hours to get the job done, with 50–60 hour working weeks now fairly commonplace. These extra hours are unpaid, whereas in the past they would have attracted overtime rates. So the average pay per hour worked has declined since 1970.

How have we not noticed this? There are several reasons why this is the case.

1. The rise of two parent working

In 1970, the average household contained one income earner, usually the man of the house. That one income had to provide everything that the family needed. The amazing thing is that the one income usually was enough, even if not much was left over to save. Fast forward to forty years later, and most families now have more than one income earner. It is a major choice for a parent to give up work to look after the children, even if the other one is working. Household budgets just won't stretch far enough. Declining real incomes increasingly mean both parents having to work.

2. The relaxation of credit controls

In 1970, there were very few people running into debt. The old joke about bank managers used to be that, if you asked to borrow money, he would look into your eyes, and only if he thought you didn't need the money would he relent and let you have it! In the last forty years, however, we have seen a transformation with banks and financial services institutions falling over each other to offer us more ways of getting ourselves into debt. With the extension and relaxation of credit cards and bank loans, you can run up as large a debt as you want without anyone really noticing. Credit card debt has disguised the decline in real income, because we can still buy what we want to anyway.

3. Home ownership and property purchase
In 1970, most people would have held the view that the way to future prosperity was to work hard and save hard. In the intervening years however, the view shifted, and we were encouraged to 'speculate to accumulate.' So the dream many people had of owning their own home was turned into the idea that 'if I buy a house, its value will rise, and I will make money.' Of course, rising house prices don't benefit us much if the price of every other house also rises. But still people have bought the idea that a house is an investment that will make money.

Indeed, many have been encouraged in the last twenty years into the 'buy to let' market, the idea of buying a second house to rent out, or to buy a holiday home to rent out to holidaymakers. Again, the hope is to make a fast buck. Often the hope proves futile.

The one thing that is guaranteed with all these property purchases is that there has been a huge rise in mortgage debt. The truth is that most houses are not privately owned. They are owned by the banks, and we are paying them to live in 'our' houses.

4. Stock market speculation
Since the 1980's, in both the UK and the US, we have seen major privatisations of industries. Privatisations have been characterised by Governments selling the assets for less than they are worth. The public have subscribed to buy up shares, with the knowledge that they could make a quick killing. Share prices have often doubled on privatisation, almost overnight, and people have made a tidy profit. Similarly, with the transfer of former building societies into the banking sector, those holding building society accounts were 'rewarded' with thousands of pounds in exchange for voting to turn their building society into a bank. Once again, you've guessed it, another opportunity to make money.

All these money making opportunities have been taken, and this has disguised the underlying decline in real incomes for most employees. Ironically, as the emphasis on making money has taken hold among the population, less physical money has actually been made. Money is often now not a physical thing anymore. Those purple, brown and blue notes have largely disappeared, replaced by online bank accounts and direct debits. To most intents and purposes, money is just a set of numbers on a piece of paper, computer screen or mobile phone. What's more, we've learned not to trust what we see on that piece of paper or screen. Just ask anyone who has read their pension statements over the last twenty years, only to discover that their pension is not worth that much anymore.

So what is money, if it no longer exists? Who makes what nowadays? No one manufactures anymore, so what is it we are making when we work? And why should those at the top earn so much more? Why should their living standards have risen so steeply over the last forty years when everyone else has largely lost out?

There is a more fundamental question. If two parent working, the relaxation of lending and credit, the rise of property purchases and stock market speculation have all largely been a ruse that disguised the decline in incomes, then what will the next confidence trick be? With Governments now saddled with huge debts to fund as a result of bailing out the banks, there is some evidence that our existing economic system may have run out of tricks to play. Just how long should we be expected to put up with this?

The current crisis

Richard D Wolff, an eminent economist with close links to Harvard, Stanford and Yale Universities, has postulated that the current economic crisis in the West is not a financial crisis. It is a larger crisis arising as a direct result of the Capitalist system running out of tricks to play. He confirms that, in the USA, average wages stopped rising post-1970 for a number of reasons - computerisation, greater foreign competition particularly in manufacturing, more women entering the workforce, and large scale immigration. He also charts the rising scale of debt, as people took out unsecured loans to fund their pattern of consumption. (6)

There are many ways in which the System of society we live under lets us down. So that leaves a big question – how do we choose to put up with it? Let's look at how this happens; starting with what it is the System needs from us.

The System's needs

The System of society is like a spoiled child, in that it runs best when it has our attention. It runs in such a way as to preserve itself, and not in a way that's best for us. When we focus our attention on the System, we are sucked in to playing the game. Society may have to suck harder with some people than with others, but essentially most of us end up going along with the game as it is.

The System has ways of making us pay attention. Nowadays, the prime cheerleader roles for the System lie with politicians, the media, and the education system. We're going to look at each of these players in more detail. Before we proceed, it's worth saying that this analysis is not aimed at criticising the actions *per se* of politicians, the media and educationalists. Most people in my experience are genuinely attempting to do a good job. In many, though not all, cases they are playing the game either sub-consciously or even unconsciously. In other words, they are not even aware that they are doing it, in the same way as we are not aware of what's going on for us for much of the time.

With this proviso, let's look at each of these areas in more detail.

Politicians

Politicians do not run the show, as is popularly supposed in a democracy. In many ways, it is more accurate to say they respond to the show. They are among the prime cheerleaders, and they instigate one of the main ways the System uses to control us. This is the role of the crisis. Politicians love crises. Without them, they would have nothing to do! Crises, as we shall see, have the effect of encouraging most people to comply with what's going on. Those who rebel, however they choose to do so, often become the 'enemy.'

Politics has become dumbed-down over the last forty years to the point where it's hard to tell the difference between the major political parties. That is no surprise when they are largely funded by the same people, by big business, and where they see running a country as not that different to running a company. Whether it's UK Ltd or USA Plc, electing the Government feels not that different to electing just another faceless Board of Directors as a shareholder. Elections are dominated by sound bites and slogans while an increasingly disenfranchised electorate turn their attention elsewhere. Part of that attention turns to TV and the media, which is of course the second cheerleader for the System.

The media

For media, read mainly TV, though we do still have magazines and newspapers – with an increasing media presence online. We've already referred to the dumbing-down of TV output with soaps and virtual reality programmes, along with the sensationalisation and trivialisation of issues that should be serious ones. The role of the media has long been stated as being 'to inform, educate and entertain.' The BBC's Royal Charter makes exactly this statement in the last renewal in 2006. (7) So we now turn to the inform part.

George Orwell in his book *1984* (8) foresaw large TV screens with news on, and this has transpired with 24-hour news programmes. The news is all around us no matter where we look. In a bank, our office, the shopping centres and railway stations, we are continually being informed of what's going on in the world. Of course, bad news sells better than good news. I don't know why, but it doesn't matter why. What happens as a result is an incessant drum roll of bad news stories. Crises here, war there, murder and crime, and at times over-hyped political controversies. If we're not careful, we are inundated by bad news.

This in turn has one main impact. We are worn down to a position of accepting our lot, because it's a lot better than it could be. I mean, just look at all this bad news! Better not rock the boat just now, because there's a recession on. Better not complain about being strip searched at the airport because, well, there are terrorists out there. Better not trust anyone because they might do me some harm! If politicians strut around on the stage to get our attention on behalf of the System, the media act as arguably the prime cheerleader for the System – its aim being to keep our attention on the 'game.' If we're not aware are of it, we are sucked in to playing the game, like good boys and girls.

To illustrate this point, let's consider the news headlines on a particular day, in this case 28th August 2014. The following is a selection of the main headlines from the BBC News website.

Rotherham victim gives her account

Russia pressed over Ukraine fighting
Depression in cancer 'overlooked.'
UK Jews and Muslims issue peace call
US hostage mother makes video plea
Ebola outbreak 'will get worse.'
Brazil pursues Amazon 'destroyers.'
Cop crew member killed by US police

On the same day, in the USA, Fox News posted the following headlines among other equally depressing ones:

Al Qaeda magazine hints at looming attack on US
West Point reports describes ISIS crisis as 4 years in the making
2nd American killed with ISIS in Syria
Pain at the pump - costly new gas taxes
Hackers reportedly hit JP Morgan
War on religion: Atheists launch attack
Russia firing missiles inside Ukraine
CEO faces anger over kicking a puppy
UN Security Council calls for cease-fire in Libya
Military jet crashes in Virginia

Do you get the message? It doesn't matter whether you look at newspapers, news websites, or watch TV. You find the same crisis-fuelled, fear-inducing, attention-grabbing mix of events to suck you in and grind you down. It's hard to be creative, fearless and inspirational in this environment. It's also harder to think clearly too.

Education

The primary role of education is to get you a job. Ever since universal education was introduced in the Victorian era, this has been the case. The only traditional exception to this is the privileged minority, who could go to private school, followed by an ancient university and study what they liked. But for this minority, getting a job was never going to be an issue. Accordingly, schools tend to run along manufacturing lines, because that is how most of industry used to run. Sir Ken Robinson, one of the foremost thinkers on education, points out that the most important factor with any child is their age – or, as he calls it, their 'date of manufacture.' Kids are batched together with other kids the same age as if it's the only thing that matters. Small issues like their motivation, their interests and preferred ways to learn

35

are largely given lip service in this batch manufacturing process. Children leave school for University or work with a 'certificate of (hopefully) competence.' Hence the obsession with qualifications, even if they don't always come with common sense! (9)

We now appear to treat education as a privatised commodity – only the individual being educated gets any benefit out of it, so charges are increasingly being introduced. Are we really saying that society doesn't benefit from this, and should therefore pay nothing? That is the road we are currently on. The System we live under sees people as 'economic units' more than anything else, and education increasingly reflects this priority.

With increasing numbers of higher education students being expected to pay their own fees, this near obsession with future employment has taken another step forward. Now there's nothing wrong with developing a range of skills that will help you get a job after graduating or leaving school. But is this the only thing that matters? I wonder whether the Ancient Greeks had a better idea of what education should be about, to teach people how to think properly. Where is the socially responsible citizen in all this?

Who benefits from the System?

If we have a System and a game we're sucked into playing, who gains from it? What is the pay-off? The answer is 'it depends on how you look at it.' Most radical thinkers would point out that the rich gain from the System. So their argument goes, the people at the top (i.e. the rich and powerful) are out to promote and reinforce their own position. Hence the often absurd attempts to justify huge pay rises for Chief Executives and senior managers, even when their businesses are performing poorly.

For example, in June 2014, the US website Fortune.com reported the five companies that were worst offenders when it came to giving pay and perks rises to CEO's, despite their poor performance. These offenders included the game maker Hasbro, 3D Systems (a printing company) and Staples (an office supply company). (10) Meanwhile, in November 2012, the *Guardian* newspaper reported that salary take home pay for senior bosses in the UK had risen by 27% in the preceding year. The *Guardian* quoted an Income Data Services report for the FTSE100 companies. This trend has continued since, and there is no evidence that the years of austerity the rest of us have had to endure has been in any way reflected in the pay of senior people - arguably the very people who created the crisis in the first place. (11)

36

Politicians don't often lose out through the System either, and those who take the decisions to axe the pension levels of the rest of the population don't usually axe their own ones at the same time. The pensions of both politicians and executives have been largely maintained. This would summarise the radical, socialist or even communist view of who gains from the System.

If we take this explanation at face value, and take the UK and US as the playing field, there are only at most 1-2 million people who run the show. What about the other 370 million or so who aren't in this position? Why do we choose to put up with the game? We'll return to this point shortly. But first, I want to focus on this privileged minority, and there are two points I'd like to make.

The first is that they are, like most of us, unaware of the game going on. They are no more aware of their role in the System's game than the rest of us are. With this lack of awareness, they simply default to playing the role the System expects of them. The second point is that the rich and powerful are often as unhappy as the rest of us, despite being economically well off. What's more, they can't hide behind the thought that 'if only I had more money, then I'd be happy.' They have all the money they need, and they've discovered that money doesn't deliver happiness as a right. In addition, many people who are outwardly successful live in perpetual fear of being 'found out.' Being 'found out' means being revealed as an imposter, fraud, or as incompetent. Their outward success conceals an inner sense of inadequacy and even desperation. This rich and powerful person might also fear that other people don't like them precisely because they are wealthy, or that their friends only like them because they are wealthy.

Given all these fears, insecurities and realisations, you have a cocktail of reasons why even the comparatively well off may not be happy. They may look like they run the game to the rest of us. However, they are part of the same game as us, even if they play on the face of it a more important or significant role on the stage. My conclusion from all this is that, whatever the solution is to society's ills, it is not resolvable through the politics of envy or jealousy. There is not a conspiracy theory we can follow here – most people are not conscious enough of the game to make it a conspiracy.

So just what is the pay-off from playing the game? Most people may feel more secure, the 'better the devil you know' syndrome. But doesn't that belief come from the System in the first place? After all, if we are all raised to feel unworthy, and just a cog in a wheel, with all the expectations that are foisted on us, then we learn to just settle for what we've got. We live in a society in which the cheerleaders instil fear as a primary motivator in each of us; the fear of not finding work; the fear of being burgled or attacked by terrorists; the fear of not making ends meet; the fear of recession. Just where did hope go in all this?

I doubt whether many people gain from playing this game. But most of us still end up doing so because we have been conditioned to play it. That's why most of us put up with it. The trouble is we put up with it at the expense of our own humanity and development as individual human beings. We put up with it by sacrificing our potential as people, our hopes and aspirations - or at least we confine our aspirations to economic ones, like buying a bigger house.

As an illustration of this, just consider the issues that dominated the Scottish independence referendum. Whatever your view on the issue, one thing is undeniable in terms of the debate that took place between 'Yes Scotland' and 'Better Together.' It was completely dominated by economic issues and one question in particular:

- Would you (and possibly your children) be better off in an independent Scotland, or as part of the United Kingdom?

"Better off" was almost exclusively couched in economic terms, with fear being whipped up by both sides. The 'Yes' campaign played on the Scots fear of never-ending Conservative Governments in the UK that would run down the welfare state and National Health Service. The 'no' campaign focused on the implications of leaving the Union on job losses, and Government tax revenues. The 'what currency will Scotland use' question was perhaps the biggest issue. The quality of debate was generally depressing, uninspiring and economic in nature.

In the end, we all sit here paying attention to the 'spoilt child' System and its cheerleaders. By doing so, we are giving the System all it needs, and we are sucked into playing the game. It doesn't mind a few rebels, as they provide the enemy, and they are after all giving the System the attention it craves.

Whose fault is it? The power of non-awareness and denial

Increasing frustration at the futility of trying to change things leads on naturally to one of society's key games, the blame game. Whose fault is it that things are so bad? Who is responsible for the corruption that exists? Who caused the inequalities that so many are afflicted by? We seek to look somewhere to assign blame for whatever it is. We blame all sorts of people – politicians, do-gooders, the workshy, bankers, Europe, immigrants, the English, terrorists, teachers, social workers, and so on. We become all judgmental with other people, and especially with people we don't know personally.

I hope you can see how counterproductive this behaviour is. We adopt one of the key components in society's game to try to change it. Can anyone see the inherent contradiction in that? The truth is that, to some extent, no-one is to blame. Most people, as we have seen, are largely unconscious of the play that we're all a part of. We play the game. Some play the game charitably, some uncharitably, many play it with bitterness, but we play it all the same. The rich did not cause this, nor did bankers, and nor did anyone else. Most simply act out the roles they fall into and the game continues.

Consider the rich businessman, who thinks nothing of closing an office because of the need to 'save money', throwing hundreds or thousands of people out of work. The result is misery, poverty, loss of self-esteem, and so on. That same businessman may well go home, head out to a charity raising function, and donate large sums of money. Rich philanthropists are at the extreme end of this spectrum. It's stating the obvious that such people are not bad. They are unaware of the play they are in, and do some good where they think they can. Oh, and they're probably not very happy either!

If we think about it, those at the top have few friends. They have lots of sucker uppers, but few friends. Who can your friends be when you're Prime Minister or President? Who do you confide in when you're running a blue chip company? We see this too in lottery winners, who end up concluding that all that money they won didn't end up making them happier. In fact, they may be even less happy than the rest of us who can still fantasise that all our problems could be washed away by one huge injection of cash!

We are all pieces in a huge game of chess. Most of us end up being pawns, but even the kings have to live in perpetual fear of being checkmated.

Some of us have nicer parts in the game, but that doesn't make us any freer for as long as we are tied into it.

I am non-aware too!

Here is another example of how easy it is to be non-aware, and it comes from me while writing this book!

In my first draft of this section, when referring to the way we become judgmental, I actually used the words "this is stupid." Realising this, I removed the words, replacing them with less judgmental ones. But then I realised that this is a great example of just what I'm talking about in this chapter. How easy is it to fall into approval and disapproval in the System we live under? The System's power is that we are so often unaware of the power it holds over us. There are times, clearly, when I share that lack of awareness!

As Jesus might have said, "forgive them, they know not what they do." The truth is, most of us don't know. However, here's the twist. Once we do become aware of the game we play in, it can never be the same. Then we do have a conscious choice about what to do. It becomes our responsibility to do something about it, if we think it should change. Once we start to move from lack of awareness and denial of our role in perpetuating the game, we can start to make different decisions.

Becoming self-aware then is the first step. But it is only the first one. There are other elements to the System's recipe that cements its control over many of us. At the root of it is the feeling that we see ourselves as small, insignificant and often crap, in comparison to what appears to be an all-powerful System. There are various aspects to this feeling, which we'll go on to explore in the next chapter. So just why do we connive in a game that gives us so little in return?

Chapter 3 – Our connivance in this game

- *Insanity in individuals is something rare – but in groups, nations, parties and epochs, it is the rule – **Friedrich Nietzsche***

Why do we connive in this game as individuals? In this chapter, we will consider four key reasons why we end up conniving in the game. First, the System itself feels very powerful, which leads us to be more inclined to submit to its grip. Second, because the option of rebelling seems a futile one. Third, because the System is adept at generating a strong sense of unworthiness in us. Fourth, because we have a strong social tendency to become assimilated.

Let's consider each of these factors in turn.

1. The System feels powerful

Let's start by looking at a day in my life, to illustrate the hold our System has over us. It wasn't a particularly eventful day, between Christmas and New Year a few years ago now.

I did what many people do during this time. I popped out to the food shop to buy our weekly groceries, having emptied the contents of my fridge, freezer and larder during the Christmas festivities. As I went about my store shopping, three things came to my attention.
1. A newspaper headline, "Britain on terror alert for New Year" shouted out at me from the newspaper stand.
2. Masses of people running round the supermarket in a locust like frenzy. It was as if they were all preparing for the seven years of famine, as talked about in the Old Testament.
3. An older man, out of the blue, suddenly saying to me "I hope it doesn't snow, as the weather men say it will".

So what did I notice about these three random events, small in themselves? First, I noticed the emphasis on dread and terror in the newspaper headline. The media mantra of "bad news is good news because it sells copies" means over-emphasising bad news. While I don't know anyone who actually lives in fear of a terrorist attack personally (maybe I just know the wrong people!), bad news doesn't encourage us to be in a good mood, or feel good about life. Secondly, the shops will re-open in a couple of days' time, so there is no need to shop as if our lives depend on it. Finally, when is snow a crisis? Many people actually enjoy having snow. But then they are probably child-like types, who like nothing better than a snowball fight!

Just how easy it is to spend our time living in fear and dread of what might happen? It is also easy to be duped by others into living this way. What does fear and dread do? Why it leads us to pull in our horns, settle for what we've got, and accept the devil we know. We shut down, give up on our dreams, become more cynical, and live with a very short term focus. There are strong forces within our society that drive us to a place of fear and dread. It is a place where we risk ceasing living, and start to merely exist.

As we saw from the behaviour in the store, there are many people who simply succumb to this game, in that the System's rules have a 'hold' on them. There are many people out there who hold to the belief that "the rules are the rules. We cannot change them. It's the order of things."

Another factor is simply that we're mortgaged up to our eyeballs in debt. It's hard to think about changing a System we owe so much to, while feeling that we're invested in it. Playing on all of these factors allows the System to gain compliance from most of us, most of the time. That is all the System needs to thrive. Record levels of Graduate, mortgage and credit card debt fuel fears that many of us have that one day we will be ruined. We will run out of money. That insecurity fuels compliance big-time.

For most of us, our part in the game becomes 'play it safe.' In this sanitised rational world, we make our decisions with our head, and not with our heart. But we also make those decisions with our compliant head on, the way our parents and early year's authority figures taught us. Compliance from the majority is understandable, even if the result is a miserable, coping life at best.

2. The futility of rebellion

However, the System has more in store for those who decide to challenge and question, to agitate for change. Many natural rebels become demoralised by the futility of opposition. This should not be a surprise. Trying to oppose the dominant forces in society is a near waste of time. 'Being against' what's going on does not work. Standing up for change usually fails, as we saw earlier from the lessons of Barack Obama, the 1945

UK Labour Party and the 2010 Liberal Democrats. More radical push-backs have largely failed too. Even movements like the Hippies in the 1960's, as we will go on to see, failed to make the change they sought.

Let's consider this point about rebellion for a moment. It is clear that compliance with a System isn't going to change it. But could rebellion change it instead? As much of modern history has shown, rebellion against the entrenched power in the System is generally futile. That's because the System needs rebels and the occasional rebellion in order to survive - possibly even to thrive.

The System arms itself with opposition as a means of deflecting attention from its own shortcomings. Sometimes, there may be justification on the face of it in viewing someone as an 'enemy.' However, the way our System does it is more about preserving itself, rather than any ideal of democracy or liberty.

For one example, just consider the case of the Muslim Cleric Abu Qatada. He preached from a mosque in the Finsbury Park area of London. More specifically, he preached the doctrine of holy war against the West. There are two points to make here. First, he was deported to Jordan to stand trial, as he was apparently wanted there on charges connected to terrorism. Guess what? Having been deported and standing trial in Jordan, he was acquitted on both counts, with the judge dismissing the evidence against him as 'weak and inadmissible.' (1) In other words, the UK fought a ten year battle to deport him with the support of the USA and much of Europe, for what amounted to very little. Certainly, it was nothing that could secure a conviction. You can also be sure that if the British government had thought they could convict him in this country, they would have gone ahead and done so!

That leads to my second point. Just look at how much noise and fanfare this news story carried for much of the ten year deportation battle. It was all over the news, with headlines of terrorism, and politicians falling over each other to be seen as tough, and to demonise him. He was repeatedly imprisoned and released in the United Kingdom after he was first detained under anti-terrorism laws in 2002, but was not prosecuted for any crime. Contrast the political and media hubbub at the time with the near deafening silence that accompanied his acquittal in Jordan. The System does not want you to know that it got things wrong.

Now, I'm not saying that Qatada is in any way justified in things he may have said about the attacks in the USA in 2001 and London in 2005. However, he clearly did not break the law. If he had, he would have been tried and convicted. The point about a democracy is that people are generally allowed to express their views, even if not pleasant views. What I am saying is that the System demonised the man to keep the rest of the population compliant in the face of the terrorist threat. The System inflated the threat from Qatada to create an enemy as a means of propping itself up.

For a more sanguine example, just consider the case of Julian Assange, after WikiLeaks exposed US military secrets. Within months of the furore, Assange was being pursued over alleged sexual indiscretions in Sweden. Again, he may have a case to answer, but isn't it a coincidence that the allegations surfaced at precisely the time when the US Government were looking for a way to 'get' Assange. Such was the move from politicians against him that the Australian Prime Minister accused Assange of breaking the law, only to be told later that he hadn't done so (Assange being an Australian.) US Vice President Joe Biden reputedly called him a 'terrorist' (the word of the decade), while a former Governor of Arkansas called for the assassination of Assange, as his conduct was on a par with a terrorist. Just imagine how Abu Qatada would have been treated had he said something similar to this!

Rebellion and compliance - how the System uses rebellion

In 2003, the largest demonstrations in UK history took place. London and Glasgow both saw the largest demonstrations of all time, alongside many smaller demonstrations in other UK cities. Millions of people marched on that day. I was one of them, and it felt at the time that people power might prove unstoppable.

It wasn't.

The marches were against the planned invasion of Iraq by the USA and Britain, supposedly to rid the country of weapons of mass destruction. With the benefit of hindsight, we now know that the weapon of mass destruction argument was a lie designed to justify regime change. However, let's not go there. I want to illustrate a different point instead.

At the time of those marches, there was huge public opposition to the war, and outside of Government circles, there wasn't much appetite for war.

However, just look at what happened when the war actually started. Once the 'Shock and Awe' bombing began and the soldiers began to arrive, public opinion swung behind the war. Opposing it became a minority pursuit. I should know, because I continued to oppose it, and very few people I knew at the time actually agreed with me! Public opinion swung behind the idea of 'supporting our boys.'

In compliance terms, it's simple. Once the System decided on war, majority opinion swung round to compliance. It stayed there for the duration, despite mounting evidence that the weapons of mass destruction did not exist. There you have it - the System uses crisis and war to induce a docile, compliant response from most of the population. That is precisely what it got, along with a few rebels who became the enemy. The System welcomed them too - it needs a show to stop the rest of us from seeing what's really going on. It uses rebellious people to bring out the judgmental qualities in the rest of us, so we don't realise that what we're doing is simply complying with the System.

Oh, and to be fair, many of the actors and actresses acting on behalf of the System don't see what's going on either! They just act out their part in the play.

The futility of conventional revolution

Of course, some rebellions do succeed in over-throwing the old 'regime.' However, it has proved much harder to overthrow the System. One of two things generally happens. First, the entrenched powers in society hijack whoever is in charge now. Second, the power vacuum breaks down completely, and there is a fight for power. For a modern example of entrenched power breaking down completely, look no further than Yugoslavia, where national groups ripped each other to shreds in a bloody series of wars over a number of years in the early 1990's. The trouble with power vacuums is that our behaviour is so entrenched just now that the same set of authoritarian behaviours kicks in, minus the old pecking order. The lesson arising from these failures is clear. We have to move away from approaches that look to other people to 'lead' change, and come to terms with the idea of playing a part in leading it ourselves. Passive hope is not an option that will go anywhere, apart from disappointment at best.

3. We feel unworthy too often

The System is very skilled at generating a strong sense of unworthiness in each of us. In a society that emphasises compliance and judgment of others, it's not a surprise to find so many people feeling unworthy about themselves and who they are. The epidemics of stress, depression and substance abuse are testimony to this lack of self-esteem. Add to this the pressure that most of us feel on resource and time, and it becomes easy to tuck our horns in and not challenge what's going on. How many of us utter those near-immortal words "I don't have the time" or "I cannot afford to take the risk." Bombarded by those twin messages endemic in society, we live our lives deferring to fear rather than living in hope. The System also imbues us with many uncertainties and phobias, including fear of failure, playing safe, the fear of being found out to be inadequate, and the feeling that in some way we are inadequate anyway.

One dimension of inadequacy that is well-researched in the modern era is the phenomenon of imposter syndrome. It exists in modern life in epidemic proportions - and yet most of us are completely unaware of it!

Imposter syndrome

Imposter syndrome is simply blame culture in reverse. Instead of blaming other people, we blame ourselves for being inept. That's why people with low self-esteem often end up blaming everyone else for things that go wrong, an attempt to disguise their own perceived inadequacy. However, one difference between the two is that Imposter syndrome focuses on the future, whereas the blame game is more concerned with the past. So with Imposter syndrome, we berate ourselves for being inept and believe we will be found out in the future. With blame game, we berate other people's ineptness for what they did in the past.

You might think that being successful would help combat imposter syndrome. Wrong! Paradoxically, the more successful we are outwardly, the bigger the imposter syndrome becomes. We fear we are not worthy of the awe in which we're held, and that this huge gap between perceptions and reality is surely going to be discovered someday soon. Then, one day something goes wrong, and we are indeed found out – and possibly face the blame game from everybody else. And so the game goes on.

This means that the rich often have a greater degree of imposter syndrome than the rest of us. The main reason for this is the greater gap between outward success and inward feelings of inadequacy. That's one reason why we see so many suicides among the rich and famous. Talented people like Amy Winehouse illustrate this point all too clearly. Paradoxically, had she been less successful, she might have still been alive today. But then Imposter Syndrome would have been less of a factor.

4. Our assimilation inclination

We human beings do have a habit of trying to impersonate each other. From fashion following to learning from others we see as successful, we creatures are definitely predisposed to impersonate others. I suspect that part of the reason for impersonating others is that we feel unworthy in our own right, as a result of the way the System behaves towards us. Whatever the cause, this impersonation does have profound consequences for each of us, and for us all collectively.

Group think

It was Friedrich Nietzsche who said that insanity in individuals was rare, but in groups of people it is the rule. Group think illustrates why this is the case. Basically, there is a tendency for people, when in the same place long enough, to converge in the ways they think and in what they believe. In other words, we start believing the same things. What's more, it becomes a stronger trend in times of crisis, and bad decisions end up getting made as a result.

The phenomenon of Group Think originated in work by psychologist Irving Janis to describe how groups can fall into this trap. (2) Group members defer to the desire for conformity and group harmony, and in the process of doing so they suspend critical judgment of the factors underpinning decisions made by the group. In so doing, they effectively sign up to ineffective, dysfunctional and even disastrous decisions. Any dissenting voices are suppressed within the group, and any contradictory voices from outside the group are ignored, suppressed or vilified.

At the same time, the qualities that might have resulted in better decisions are undermined. These include individual creativity, uniqueness and independent thinking. These are the very qualities that, as we'll go on to see, are discouraged by the dominant System game.

The group becomes over-confident of its own invulnerability in making good decisions, and ignores the opinions of 'outsiders,' who are often dehumanised as the 'enemy.' Does this all sound familiar to you? It should do, but now let's look at the consequences of this. The give-away signs of Groupthink include the following non-exhaustive list: (3)

- Illusions of invulnerability creating excessive optimism and encouraging risk taking.
- Rationalising warnings that might challenge the group's assumptions.
- An unquestioning belief in the morality of the group, causing members to ignore the consequences of their actions.
- Stereotyping those who are opposed to the group as weak, evil, biased, spiteful, disfigured, impotent, or stupid.
- Direct pressure to conform placed on any member who questions the group, couched in terms of "disloyalty".
- Self-censorship of ideas that deviate from the apparent group consensus.
- Illusions of unanimity, with silence being viewed as agreement.

Group think becomes more significant when groups are highly cohesive and when they are under considerable pressure to make a quality decision. It can also, as we will see, occur on a team, organisational or even a national (or international) scale.

Now all this might sound a bit academic. Let's bring it to life with some examples of where Group think has produced poor decisions at every level.

Team Group think

One of the best examples of Group think occurred with the NASA Space Shuttle disaster in 1986, when the Challenger exploded in the sky, killing all astronauts on board. The investigation afterwards into what happened revealed that the team responsible for deciding when to launch suppressed concerns about safety when under pressure to get the Shuttle into the sky. In particular, engineering concerns about some of the seals were overridden, and those same engineers signed up to the launch decision despite their misgivings.

Group think highlights the risk that we as human beings end up going along with insane ideas. The extreme example of this is Nazi Germany, with millions of civilised people signing up to a murderous, evil regime, an unwinnable war, and the eventual partition of their own country. No German, thinking on his or her own, would have come up with such a plan (apart from Hitler himself.)

Organisational Group think

Groupthink has the capacity to undermine entire organisations. One modern example of this was the decline of Kodak from being a company synonymous with cameras to its demise when filing for bankruptcy in January 2012. It was largely destroyed by its failure to deal with the explosion of digital cameras in the last twenty years, and the near collapse of any mass market for film cameras.

Yet it was an employee of Kodak that invented the digital camera in the first place! All the way back to the late 1970's, a Kodak engineer Steve Sasson invented the digital camera, which he christened 'filmless photography.' Not only this, but Kodak patented the digital camera in 1978. However, this was followed by precisely nothing. From 1983-93 Kodak senior managers, who were raised in the Kodak style, prioritised high earning film cameras over low earning rates for digital cameras. Even when it became clear that the company strategy was wrong, the legacy Kodak management culture got in the way of any successful action being taken.

The result was that, instead of cementing its legacy in the camera market, Kodak cemented its own destruction.

National Group think

Group think also has the potential to infect the decision making of entire nations. For two more recent examples, if more modest than the German one, look to the British decision to invade Iraq, and the Scottish independence referendum. In both cases, they encapsulated the power of a political team to succumb to Group think, and spark a similar transition in large sections of a national population inspired by national security and nationalism respectively.

Prior to the 2003 UK invasion of Iraq with the USA, public opinion was largely against going to war. The Labour Government, under Tony Blair, had effectively committed to going to war long before the record public demonstrations that took place throughout the UK. The Government ignored informed 'outside' opinion that questioned whether Saddam Hussein possessed any weapons of mass destruction. Outside opinion included Hans Blix, the Head of the UN Weapons Inspectorate at the time. Other voices were ignored by both British and American Governments, notably the French who made clear they would veto any UN resolution legitimising any invasion.

The power of Group think was highlighted by the departure of Robin Cook from the British Government in 2003. As the one senior dissenting voice in the room, he saw the futility of staying in a room where he was unheard. He chose to become an 'outsider.'

As mentioned earlier in this chapter, the 2003 invasion was a great example in itself of the way most people end up complying with the System. Group think is a significant factor behind such cases of compliance. As soon as the first bombs were dropped, public opinion swung behind the invasion. This was a case of mass compliance at its best, reinforced by the usual mantra of "supporting our boys in action." Of course, we don't get to choose whether they are thrown into action in the first place.

This was a great example of national Group think. It happened in the USA too. Does anyone now care to remember the re-christening of 'French fries' that took place, after the traitorous French refused to back the invasion? Why, they were re-named "freedom fries." Does that recollection make you wince now? That's what happens with national Group think!

A similar occurrence took place with the 2014 Scottish independence referendum campaign. On one side was a tightly organised 'Yes' campaign, coordinated by the Scottish National Party Government. They were a closely knit group sharing a common bond, and led by a strong leader in Alex Salmond. They were opposed by a loose coalition of parties and groups, whose one common thread was a desire for Scotland to remain within the UK. In this scenario, Group think could only really occur on one side - and it did.

It occurred to the extent that warnings from other eminently well-qualified people on issues as diverse as currency union, implications for the Scottish financial services industry, and concerns about North Sea oil revenue were ignored and their sources ridiculed by the Scottish Government. In addition, matters like whether or not Scotland would retain its place in the European Union and NATO were sidestepped. It appeared at times as though the Scottish Government viewed all these comments as part of a great conspiracy theory – they certainly dismissed the comments without bothering to answer them beyond shooting the messenger.

However, this Group think infection was caught by large sections of the Scottish electorate, with 45% voting for independence despite none of these issues being dealt with. No doubt that was partly motivated by nationalist sentiment, and part was a huge distaste (largely understandable) at the behaviour of Westminster politicians for decades. However, walk around the streets of Edinburgh and Glasgow in the last few weeks of the campaign, and you could feel the palpable sense of hysteria, unreality and a wilful desire to ignore large tracts of information pertinent to the issue of independence. Group think may result in a group high, but that doesn't mean good decisions are made.

It's also true that this campaign was not helped by the campaign against Scottish independence, which did appear to be largely negative in nature. There wasn't enough emphasis on the importance of putting forward a positive case for Scotland remaining in the UK. The result of this was a much closer referendum result than it looked like being for most of the campaign. For much of the campaign, it looked like a choice between voting out of delusion or out of fear. That isn't a great choice.

The message is clear from all this. We might dream ourselves as being autonomous, independent unique human beings. But, in the words of that dreaded race from Star Trek fame, the Borg, we are all too often being assimilated. We choose to behave as if resistance is indeed futile.

The challenge

Our tendency to connive in the game masks one key dynamic that is in play currently. On one level we know about it, as we know about much else that's wrong with the current System. But on another level we choose to ignore the takeover that's going on right under our unconscious eyes. It is the takeover of democracy.

When we behave unconsciously, we have a tendency to become 'human photocopiers'. We simply copy other people, we copy the dominant opinions in our society, and we follow fashions. The challenge we have is to become more conscious of this fact. Once we become conscious of our tendency, we can then choose to make a choice.

Facing up to this dynamic is critical if we are to change things for the better. Later on, we will look at how we can become more self-conscious, and then make different choices. For now though, understanding the dynamics in play within our current System matters. So we are going to look at this in greater depth, starting with two ideas we hear a lot about. These ideas are capitalism and democracy, and the dominant assumption that if we want one, we must have both. It's time to explode a few more myths.

Chapter 4 – Capitalism and Democracy

- *"Insanity: doing the same thing over and over again and expecting different results"* - **Albert Einstein**

The challenge we must face up to

A ll of this brings us on to capitalism. Given the above analysis, and recent economic woes, many economists and commentators have questioned whether capitalism will survive. In my view, as things stand, it will survive. Capitalism will simply regulate scarcity and the decline in natural resources. Prices will rise. In my childhood, the joke was that, if air was scarce, capitalists would simply move to sell it in bottles. We would literally see the privatisation of the air supply!

Economists like Richard D Wolff point out that capitalism has run out of tricks to play. There are no more bubbles it can inflate to provide the illusion of prosperity. There are no future equivalents of the housing bubble, stock market bubble, or dot com bubble. Wolff correctly highlights that if we leave the basis of private enterprise as it is, we won't succeed in changing the capitalist game. He proposes a move towards industrial and business democracy, where the employee rather than shareholder becomes king. Boards of Directors would in effect be elected by employees, not shareholders. This solution does fit well with the idea of democracy - if we are supposed to be so democratic, why is democracy excluded in the area that forms the biggest part of most of our lives? Most people spend most of their waking life at work.

Wolff's solution sounds enticing, but the problem with it is that it relies on those people who control the game changing the game. They are unlikely to do this. For the same reason that political reform movements generally fail, this type of economic reform won't happen unless we make it happen. When the interests of democracy and capitalism don't coincide, the interests of the latter usually prevail.

CREATE YOUR OWN REVOLUTION

The question is not whether capitalism will survive. The question is will democracy? We have only to consider cases where democratically elected leaders in the developing world have taken on the interests of big business. More often than not, they have ended up by being deposed, or worse.

In traditional Western thinking since 1945, capitalism and democracy have been synonymous. But one of them has been the dominant partner. We may be about to find out just how dominant.

It's either that, or we have a choice to make.

The post-1945 capitalist story has been a seductive one. I myself fell for that seduction while studying Economics at Glasgow University. The story runs something like this. Capitalism provides consumers with choice. Choice is good. Therefore capitalism is good. Socialism and Communism don't work because they provide no choice – either in goods and services, or in Governments. You get what you are told you can have. So the Socialist-Communist goal of equality doesn't work either, because even if you get it, it will only be an equality of mediocrity. In the worst case scenario, we end up with an equality of tyranny.

Capitalism is unequal, but two great features about the System justify this. First, the System rewards risk takers, innovators, and those who 'work hard.' In other words, if there is inequality, it can be explained in a way that justifies it. If you work hard, you can make it. Capitalism rewards those who come up with new products that will make our lives better. So, if people take risks, they deserve all the rewards they can get.

The second great feature, crucial to everyone buying into the capitalist story, is the notion of 'trickle down.' This is the idea that, even if those at the top get more, the benefits of capitalism will trickle down like syrup off a rich man's table, and everyone will feel the benefits, and be better off in the long run than under some other system.

This story we are told moves on seamlessly to the other twin pillar of Western society, democracy. Democracy is about choice, and free open elections provide that choice. Anyone can stand for election, and we can vote to decide who wins.

So if capitalism is about choice, and democracy is about choice, then you don't have to travel far to conclude that capitalism is essential to democracy. In a nutshell, this is the justification for why we have what we have as our System.

The myth of the free market

We saw earlier in this book how the capitalist bubble has played a number of tricks over the last forty years to convince us that we are better off, when real incomes have been at best stagnant or even declining. Essentially, it has done this by encouraging us to mortgage ourselves up to our eyeballs, as we take on increasing levels of debt. There is only so far this can go, and with the decline in natural resources we now face, it is unlikely that capitalism can continue to pull off these stunts. The inherent failings of our economic system will become increasingly obvious.

The myth of the free market lies in the idea of risk-taking. Society's dominant propaganda that it rewards and values risk-takers is backed up by what exactly? I remember the UK Chancellor of the Exchequer, George Osborne, addressing the Lord Mayor's Banquet in the City of London in 2011. During that speech, he made reference to wanting "the City of London to be a thriving centre of enterprise."

Mr Osborne, who benefitted greatly from a privileged education that meant he didn't have to take any risk himself, extolled the virtues of risk-taking, in front of a group of the richest business people in the UK. Now, I'm not jealous of people who sit in banquets like this – personally I would be bored. However, I doubt if there were many in that room who even know what taking a risk looks like. They probably delegate that job to someone else! There's a serious point here. All the evidence of how capitalism works is that it HATES the idea of risk taking. Large corporations talk about controlling risk, and markets don't like sudden change of any kind. Instead, capitalism values predictability.

Of course, there are exceptions to this, like Sir Richard Branson and Lord Sugar. But they are a small group of exceptions, compared to the often faceless corporate civil servants who run our companies, and effectively run our country too.

So if our corporations don't carry the risk, who is it that does? Guess who? Just consider what happened with the banking collapse in October

2008. When the risk of collapse became imminent, politicians were falling over each other to bail them out with public money. We must know that there is no way the banks will ever repay their debts. We all know they won't, even though most of us think they should. After all, if they were going to repay the full extent of their folly, there would have been no need to cut publicly funded programmes by as much. Why would you cut them if you knew you were going to get the money back? In this way, the George Orwell 'doublethink' game works – we say one thing, while deep down knowing that the truth is something completely different. (1) We all know the politicians are not going to make the banks repay what they owe. Politicians know that we know – hence the public anger that remains years after the banking crash. But still the game of 'we'll get our money back' goes on.

Banks and companies don't carry the risk, we do.

The hijacking of democracy

On 21st February 2014, the Independent newspaper reported that the austerity measures taken in Greece as a condition of remaining within the Euro currency zone had resulted in 1 million Greek citizens having no access to health care whatsoever. Greek hospital budgets were cut by 25% and pharmaceuticals by more than half, between 2009 and 2011. This in turn led to a surge in infant mortality rates among other consequences. (2) Meanwhile, on 13th February 2014, the BBC reported that Greece's unemployment rate had reached 28%, and its rate for the under-25's an appalling 61.4%. (3) These are truly appalling figures, and it can be no surprise that political extremism is on the rise in that country.

In a similar vein, democratically elected Governments don't run the show that is Britain, or the USA – or any other country out there. To a considerable extent, big business runs the show. In 2012, if Facebook had been a country, it would have been the 5th biggest country in the world. How much influence does that carry? So how much influence do Microsoft and Apple have? What about Unilever, Fox or Sky Broadcasting, or the large financial institutions with global presence. Aren't they more important than a lot of countries?

We've seen the scene these last few years where banks have largely got away with truly awful practices because they are seen as 'too big to fail.' That hasn't been the case with nations though. Greece, to avoid being cut adrift completely, has been required to cut its expenditure dramatically, with horrendous consequences as outlined above. Greece isn't allowed to get away with it, and they are not alone in this.

So the notion of national sovereignty is exposed as another myth, as any Greek would now tell you. A new Government can be elected, as long as it pursues the same policies. People are left with no choice. This is ironic given the number of nationalist movements that have gained momentum, even in Europe these last few years. In Scotland, Catalonia, the Basques, even in Belgium, and the ongoing fragmentation of the old Soviet Union republics with new breakaway republics. The irony is that, as the big Corporations get bigger and bigger, the size of nations and governments are going in the opposite direction. Whether small is beautiful or not is a matter for debate. But small isn't going to counteract the overwhelming power of the big corporations. We're not going to do anything about capitalism by stressing what it is that makes us different from each other.

It should come as no surprise that Corporations count for more than countries do. After all, we live in a world where money matters more than human beings do. The reality of our democracy is that political parties are increasingly funded by organisations, particularly big business, and not by individual subscriptions. Winning an American Presidential election uses up enough money to bail out a significant sized country. But companies vie with each other to buy power, and access to the President. Where the USA goes, the UK meekly follows. The leaders of our political parties increasingly look the same – but then they are largely funded by the same people. Businesses pay the party bill, and then lobby the successful candidates when in office. In whose interest are they lobbying? Probably not for ours.

At least in the West, you can argue that democracy has been hijacked by capitalism. Elsewhere in the world, democracy was strangled at birth by this same economic machine. Just look at the momentous events in 2011, with the Arab Spring uprising against the various dictatorships in the Middle East. What has that produced? In Egypt, it produced a popular uprising and the overthrow of Hosni Mubarak, virtual dictator of Egypt since the early 1980's. Elections soon followed, with Mohammed Morsi victorious. However, being a member of the Muslim Brotherhood, he was not considered an ally of the West. Given this, it was fairly predictable that he was overthrown within two years, and replaced by – you got it – a new dictator. The army overthrew Morsi amid considerable public dissent, which was then suppressed.

I'm not going to play conspiracy theories here about whether the Western powers did anything to help overthrow Morsi. It is enough to know that the Western Governments did nothing to support the democratic outcome in Egypt. I don't recall one serious protest being made from the West. Now, had Morsi been pro-West, which means in practice pro-capitalist, then the outcry would have been huge. The message is clear. Democracy is expendable; the interests of capitalism are not.

Instead of real choice over real things that matter in life, and real participation in how we are governed, the System gives us meaningless choice over meaningless things. We are consumers, not people. Our value is in what we consume, not in what we want, or who we are. We have meaningless choice at elections between options that are no different from each other. It's no wonder that most of us no longer bother voting most of the time. We are only consumers. We ceased to be human beings a long time ago.

If capitalism and democracy are partners in any sense, it is at best a marriage of convenience. But it is capitalism that wears the trousers. History, from Chile to Egypt to Greece shows that, when capitalism and democracy clash, there is only one winner.

The focus on wealth

One of the prime areas of power struggle within our capitalist society has been on wealth and in particular the distribution of wealth. This is understandable, given that money is the language that we all speak in this game of ours. In traditional politics we have the free-market Conservatives on the one hand, arguing that the key to prosperity is to let entrepreneurs have their reward, as it is the only way to raise living standards for everyone in the long run. On the other hand, left leaning Liberals and Socialists have argued to a greater or lesser degree for a redistribution of wealth as the means to achieve greater equality and reduce or eradicate poverty.

This argument has persisted for the last century or longer. In the western world, with the all-powerful global economy, it would seem like the argument has been won by the free market Conservatives. It has become hard to tell the UK Labour Party and the US Democrats apart from more conservative forces anymore. All of which is extremely dispiriting for those of us who believe in change.

However, this political power struggle has played into the hands of the System, and I believe we have taken our eye of the ball. The single biggest issue preventing a more just society is not the distribution of wealth at all. Instead, it is the distribution of power. It is power that is centralised at present in a few hands. The levers of power lie at the top of great Corporations, senior levels of Government and the media. Much of it is hidden from public view, and disguised by the language of democracy, participation, and free market choice.

Now you could argue 'chicken and egg', which came first? Maybe it does not matter. Certainly, there is ample evidence that money can buy power - just look at the donations given to political parties. But it is equally true that power can buy money. You only need to examine the way that Executive pay in Britain and the USA has been determined for much of the past twenty years to see this.

For the purposes of this book, I would suggest that it's more important to look at redistributing power. Wealth will follow the trail. What's more, we cannot rely on those in power to redistribute it, and be more inclusive. We need to find ways to empower ourselves, and redistribute it that way. How do we do this? Well, the starting point is to consider the System game a bit more. Despite its appearing to be an all-powerful juggernaut, it actually contains within it some serious weaknesses that we can take advantage of - if we can work out how to do this.

In the next chapter, we'll look at some of these weaknesses, exploring why they are weak points. From there, we'll go on to examine some strategies for dealing with these weaknesses in such a way that change becomes inevitable within the System. If we are prepared to do something about it (rather than moan), then we have the opportunity to do so.

Chapter 5 - Analysing the game

- *A great many people think they are thinking when they are merely rearranging their prejudices - **William James***

An introduction to Transactional Analysis

So far, I have focused on the System game by describing it more from a society viewpoint, with a desire to transform it. During the introduction to this book, I also talked about the need for change from a self-help perspective. Now it's time to combine the two areas, to analyse society's game using a well-established psychological approach. It is an approach that is often used in personal development, self-help and therapy. It is called Transactional Analysis or TA. (1) TA will throw light on the nature of the game that is being played. Those of you who are familiar with TA can skip straight on to the next section, where we apply its principles.

Transactional Analysis describes well how the System game works, and why it works. The first step is to describe the classical TA model. We'll then begin to apply the theory to describe what the System game involves. Later on, we will go on to look at what the implications of this game are for us as individuals, and how we live.

TA has its origins in work carried out by Dr Eric Berne. Dr Berne wrote a well-known book called 'Games People Play,' which is based on TA (2). What we will go on to see is that society plays games too – and that adherence to the System is just playing a big game. But it is a game that costs us dear. It is a game we have no chance of winning.

At the root of TA is what has commonly become known as 'parent-adult-child' theory.

The model provides a language for looking at how we interact in society with other people, and in the relationships we have with them. You don't need me to tell you that we learn how to behave, and how not to behave, from our early years in life. Our parents, relatives, teachers and other figures of authority all try to teach us lessons. We also observe how other people behave, and learn from what we see them doing and saying. What they do is more important in terms of what we learn. Hence the futility of the war cry that parents have used for centuries "don't do as I do, do as I say!" In practice, we learn more from how other people behave than from what they tell us.

Dr Berne described three 'ego states' or states of mind, for how we relate to other people. These three ego states are described as Parent, Adult and Child. 'Parent' describes our behaviour, thoughts and feelings that we copied from our parents or parental figures. It represents 'life as it is taught.' 'Adult' describes our behaviours, thoughts and feelings which are direct responses to what's going on right now. It represents life as it is thought. 'Child' is the behaviours, thoughts and feelings that we replay directly from childhood. It represents life as it is felt.

Let's look in a bit more detail at the three ego states. Our own individual motivation and behaviour is driven by these three ego states to varying degrees, as we shall see. The three ego states are depicted in the diagram below.

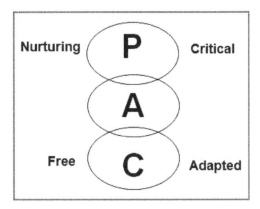

Parent

Parent represents 'life as it is taught.' In practice, the 'Parent' ego state is sub-divided between Critical Parent (CP) and Nurturing Parent (NP). Critical Parent is the part of us that judges other people against standards. It is often critical, disciplining and restrictive of other people, in some way laying down the law. Nurturing Parent is the part that looks after, or takes care of other people, taking responsibility for them in some way. It tends to be helpful, caring and loving of others.

In both 'Parent' states, it is worth emphasising that we are essentially taking responsibility for someone else – or at least trying to take responsibility. In that sense, we risk disempowering someone else (and not necessarily a child), either by being overly critical and judgmental, or by looking after someone too much or even being patronising towards them.

Adult

The Adult ego state represents 'life as it is thought'. Our Adult state is the part of us that is most like Mr Spock of Star Trek fame, tending to focus on facts rather than feelings. Our Adult state is calm and mature. When we operate from our Adult state, we are focusing on the here and now rather than being influenced by our past. Incidentally, young children are more than capable of behaving in this Adult way, often when they ask the question 'why?'

Like the 'Parent' ego state, the 'Adult' one takes responsibility for their own position. But unlike the 'Parent' state, the 'Adult' ego state does not see itself as being responsible for anyone else. When we behave in the 'Adult' state, we expect other people to take full responsibility for themselves.

Child

Our Child ego state represents life as it is felt. It too is sub-divided into two parts, Free Child (FC) and Adapted Child (AC). Free Child is the fun-loving, spontaneous part of us, not afraid to show real emotion, good or bad. It is compulsive and instinctive, and can also be undisciplined and quite demanding in nature. Adapted Child, as the name suggests, are the ways in which we adapt ourselves to authority in our lives. We learn to comply or rebel against authority, recognising that the other person is the authority. If we feel guilty, rebellious or obedient, then we are behaving from Adapted Child. One important aspect of the Child ego state is that we do not see ourselves as being responsible at the time for whatever is going on. We see someone else as being responsible, or holding the power. We simply comply with, rebel against, or react in an openly emotional, spontaneous way with whoever the authority is.

Each of us is made up to varying degrees of each of the three ego states.

How responsibility is viewed

We're talking in this book about creating our own revolution, to bring about change to our society and the dominant System. So the notion of responsibility becomes an important one, as ultimately we will need to take responsibility for ourselves and our actions to create change.

So let's consider how each ego state views responsibility.

With the Parent ego state, we view ourselves as having responsibility not only for ourselves, but also for other people. That could include our children of course, but it might also extend to our team at work. We might habitually take responsibility for organising our friend's social arrangements, and so on. This responsibility will also include responsibility for passing judgment on other people's actions, of approval and disapproval.

When we operate from Adult, that means we are taking responsibility for our own thoughts and reactions in the present moment, given the information we have. But we do not see ourselves as holding any responsibility for other people. We are likely to see them as capable of taking their own responsibility for things. We are simply taking responsibility for what we do in the present moment.

When we operate from Child, we are not seeing ourselves as responsible at all. We see others as being responsible in some way instead. With Free Child, we simply absolve ourselves from all responsibility and do what we want to do for no other reason than we want to do it! We are spontaneous. With Adapted Child, we literally adapt to someone else, whom we see as being responsible. We might comply or rebel, however either way we see someone else as being responsible.

How TA works in practice

The fun really begins when we engage with other people. When we do communicate with other people, we do so using one of these ego states at any point in time. The language we use, and how we say it, will often give away the ego state we are using at that time. To take some examples of some of the things we may say:

Don't touch that! - Critical Parent

Your performance is not up to standard - Critical Parent
Leave it to me; I'll sort it out - Nurturing Parent
You don't need to be afraid - Nurturing Parent
What do you think? - Adult
Let's see if we can solve this problem - Adult
Let's go to the pub! - Free Child
Hey, that's mine! - Free Child
That must be right because she says it is - Adapted Child
You always want me to do it that way - Adapted Child

These, of course, are just the words. This takes no account of the way in which we say it - how our tone of voice sounds, or how we look. These aspects of the message will influence which of the ego states you are using, and are seen by other people as using.

Interactions or transactions

When we speak from our Parent ego state, we are generally targeting the Child ego state in the person we are speaking to. In other words, we are looking for them to respond from their Child ego state. Let's illustrate this with an example:

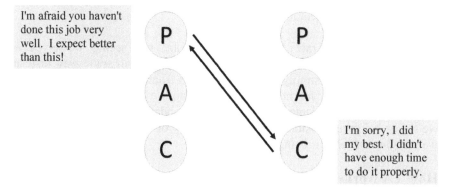

When we speak from the Adult ego state, we are targeting the adult state in the other person. Here is an example of when this happens:

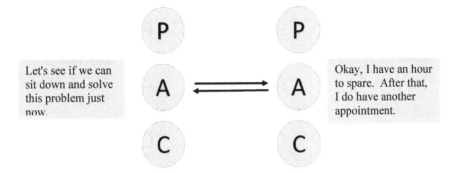

When we speak from our Child ego state, we are likely to end up targeting the Parent in the other person. Again, to illustrate by example:

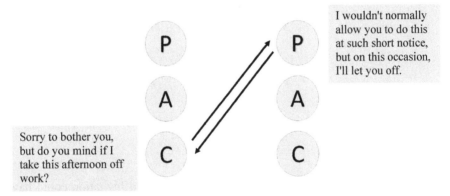

It is worth pointing out that there are some occasions where you can have either Parent-Parent or Child-Child interactions. Let's look at some examples to illustrate this.

Parent to Parent interactions usually take the form of two people talking about someone else, who isn't necessarily in the room. An example of this would be as follows.

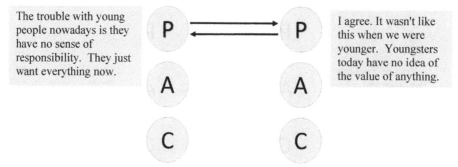

By contrast, the child - child interaction either ends up being some kind of spontaneous invitation to do something (Free Child), or a moaning or whining session (Adapted Child.) An example of the Free Child variation is outlined here.

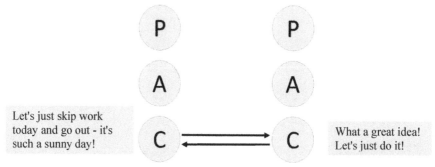

Of course, in the above example, the Free Child invitation could have been declined from the respondent's Adapted Child, for example "I'm not able to I'm afraid. My boss expects me to work this afternoon."

All of these are examples of complementary transactions, in that we get the response from the ego-state we are seeking. 'Complementary' does not mean 'good' in any way, but nor is it not good. Complementary means that the relationship as it is will continue to persist in the form it currently takes. So, for example, if the relationship is Critical Parent to Adapted Child, person A is likely to continue in the role of Critical Parent, person B in the role of Adapted Child. In this way, the relationship could continue indefinitely. That doesn't necessarily make the conversation or the relationship healthy. It just means it is likely to continue in the same sort of pattern.

In addition to 'Complementary Transactions,' there are two other types of transaction that could take place. Let's look at these before we move on, because they might spark some light on how we can generate change, thinking about our bigger questions about society.

Crossed transactions

With a crossed transaction, the person initiating the conversation does not receive the type of response they were hoping for, or expecting. Let's illustrate the crossed transaction by taking a couple of the examples I've already talked about. But in each case, there is a different ending!

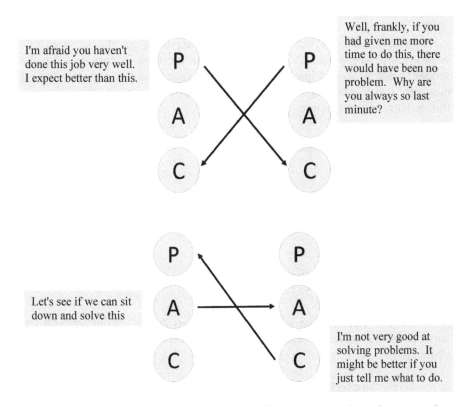

These two examples of crossed transactions show their main properties, which are as follows:

1. If person A started the conversation, person B's response is likely to prove a surprise. At the very least, it will be a disappointment.
2. They are likely to result in conflict, or a power struggle. There isn't agreement on the nature of the relationship in terms of ego states. For example, is it Parent to Child, Child to Parent, or Adult to Adult?
3. The conflict will only be resolved when a new complimentary TA relationship is established, or when the relationship breaks down completely.

As you can see, transactions can be complimentary or they can be crossed. But there is a third option. Transactions can also be ulterior - and the word provides the clue!

Ulterior transactions

With an ulterior transaction, what's happening on the surface isn't what's really going on. A social or surface message is conveyed by the sender. But a second message is also conveyed, called a psychological message. It is this message that is the real intended message. Let me illustrate this with one more example.

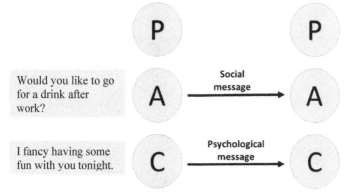

As you can see, the social message is an Adult - Adult one on the surface. However, the underlying message is a Child - Child one, of the Free Child kind!

While the psychological message is what's really meant by the message, the receiver of the message might not get the gist, and choose to believe the social message instead. Sometimes, this can simply be down to naiveté. Alternatively, they may choose to ignore the psychological message.

Ulterior transactions provide the basis for what is now called 'Game Theory' in TA. The idea behind Game Theory is that we play games with our real intentions and motives by disguising them as something else. In the above transactions, person A sets out with the game in mind. Person B might 'get the drift' and play the game back, or they might be naively unaware of what's going on. In this case, they risk falling into a trap by for example taking up the invitation for a drink as just that!

Of course, the 'drink' example is not a very good example of an ulterior transaction, as just about everyone is likely to work out what it means. The value of an ulterior transaction is that it isn't always so obvious.

*****

Of course, much of the TA approach we adopt as adults will have been learned in childhood. In particular, how we react to authority will have been established at an early age. Any parent will tell you that, at some point, they catch themselves talking to their children, and then realising that they now sound just like their own parents did! We are to a considerable extent programmed to behave in certain ways, and not in others.

We have now examined the characteristics of Parent, Adult and Child, as well as the three different types of transactions we can have. I hope you can see how this is relevant to the quality of communication we have with other people, and the quality of relationships we have in our life. However, I'm going apply TA in a different way just now. It also has significant impact on the quality of our whole society, and I want to take our attention back to the game that's going on there.

Society's game and TA

How we are brought up in our families heavily influences how we will turn out. But the families that bring us up are in turn heavily influenced by society's way of doing things - and in many ways, this influence is getting stronger.

How many of you feel like you're treated like children a lot of the time? All the emphasis is on what you can and cannot do. Even if it's not written in law, you feel pressure to behave in certain ways, and to avoid doing other things. That is because society as a whole values certain ways of behaving over others. The parent styles are actively utilised in the game, which means you are often thrust into the role of child. Consider the following scenarios.

- You are required to remove half your luggage, laptops, shoes and personal toiletries whenever you go through an airport security system.
- To get a job, you are assessed at interview, and assessed once you have got the job at appraisal meetings or performance reviews. Everyone working in any organisation reports to a 'boss' of some description.
- Experts telling us what we should and shouldn't eat, how to bring up children, how to pay taxes properly, and how to look after our health.
- Religious leaders at all levels setting out morally (or religiously) acceptable codes of behaviour.
- The nanny state interfering in all aspects of our lives, regulating everything from smoking to alcohol purchase.

Yes, you got it! Society plays the 'Parent' role well. So what happens in response? Most of us will respond in a 'Child' way, almost always Adapted Child. So we comply, rebel or try to ignore whatever is going on. We try for example to ingratiate ourselves with the boss, we comply with state rules because we'd get caught out if we didn't, and we defer to the state 'looking after' us while moaning about it.

"If it wasn't for the Government, we'd all be able to get on with things."

Often then, we get caught in 'Adapted Child.' What's more, that is the role authority expects from us. Most people will comply, a few will rebel, but Adapted Child is the dominant modus operandi.

Of course, we go through life learning from authority figures. So when we're not playing the Adapted Child role, we become quite good at adopting the Parental ego state ourselves. We put a Parent mask on. Just consider the following comments:

"Politicians are just in it for themselves. I can't trust any of them!"
"Business fat cats pay themselves far too much!"
"The conduct of the banks is a ******* disgrace!"

We ape the Parent behaviours, particularly Critical Parent, when talking to other people. We also do so when we feel in control, or we're the expert in a situation. There is no more obvious example of this than a parent telling their children off, or protecting them from harm by putting a curfew on when they can go out.

CREATE YOUR OWN REVOLUTION

The System game encourages us to play to Adapted Child and both Critical and Nurturing Parent. However, this comes at a cost - we are discouraged from both 'Adult' and 'Free Child' behaviour. The second one probably won't surprise you, but the first one might. So let's consider how this happens.

The demise of Adult and Free Child

Let's start with childhood again. Adult behaviour is motivated by the desire to find out things, to understand and question. When behaving in an Adult way, we are living in the present, and not letting either the past or future bother us too much. Children naturally do this, and what happens sooner rather than later is that this behaviour is discouraged. After all, it can be rather inconvenient to have children questioning everything all the time! How often do we hear this?
Young child: "Why is this?"
Parent: "Because I said so" or "will you stop asking questions."

Of course, we see it in adulthood too. We see it with corporate whistleblowers who notice evidence of bad or unethical practice, question what's going on, and end up paying for it with their jobs. 'Adult' behaviour is encouraged much less in our society than we might suppose. Instead, we learn not to ask questions, to turn a blind eye, and to defer to authority.

Free Child is also actively discouraged as an approach to use. The natural, spontaneous unbridled emotional approach to life is usually frowned upon, often referred to as 'immature.' People behaving in this way (even grown-ups) are often told to 'grow up' or to 'stop being so emotional.'

An illustration of society's impact

Let me graphically illustrate the impact of society on a typical individual human being, who we'll call David. David is a reasonably well-adjusted member of society, with a young family, and he takes his responsibilities seriously. In fact, he is altogether too serious, but we'll come to that shortly.

We're going to look at David by using what's known as an egogram. This is basically a graph that shows the extent to which David's behaviour in life is driven by each of the five main Ego State categories. To remind ourselves, these are Critical Parent (CP), Nurturing Parent (NP), Adult (A), Adapted

71

Child (AC) and Free Child (FC). An egogram is a bar chart, and the higher the bar for a particular ego state, the more significant that ego state is for that individual. With all this in mind, it's now time to meet David's egogram!

Meet David's Egogram

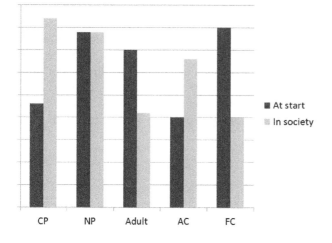

So, what do we see? The dark bars show David's natural egogram, what it looked like when he was relatively free of society's influences. As we can see, he had high Free Child, Nurturing Parent and Adult, with relatively low scores for Critical Parent and Adapted Child. In his natural state then, we see a guy who is creative and spontaneous, who likes to look after other people and take them under his wing, and who is capable of living in the 'here and now' using his Adult ego state. He can, and does, use the other two ego states at times, but Adapted Child and Critical Parent are relatively rarely used in his natural state.

What happens when we put David into the System of society, with all its pressures, expectations and challenges? These are illustrated by the grey bars, and what we see is a transformation of his personality! Now, David's strongest traits are Critical Parent, Nurturing Parent, and Adapted Child. In life, he is strongly Parental in his approach, quick to become judgmental of other people, and not just his children. This is balanced by his Nurturing Parent, which still leads to him looking after other people. Indeed, his biggest complaint about those he works with is that they don't show any initiative. That's no surprise given his Parental approach - he is encouraging Adapted Child in other people through his behaviour. Ironically, David is also deferential to authority, something he picked up from School initially, but reinforced by his experience of society and work. He is compliant and unassertive with his bosses, who complain in turn that David doesn't show much initiative!

David's low Adult and Free Child mean that genuine independent thinking, creativity and spontaneity are things that pass him by more often than not. If he raises his children this way, it's likely they will end up being more or less the same. So the System play moves on to another generation.

We can see in David the typical pattern showing the impact of society on human beings. Critical Parent and Adapted Child become stronger, as they are encouraged by the System. Free Child and Adult are relatively discouraged, and so wither on the vine. The impact of this is that David is not acting in his natural way. So he feels discontented with life, and is always tired at the end of the day. It takes a lot of energy to behave like someone else, and not the person that we are.

A positive word on the ego states

It is worth pointing out that, at this stage, it would be tempting to assume that the following is true from the above analysis:
- Parent (especially Critical Parent) = BAD
- Adult = GOOD
- Free Child = GOOD
- Adapted Child = BAD

Such a black-and-white analysis would be incorrect. Ego states are not good or bad. It's more a case of they are being over-used or under-used to play the System game we have defaulted into playing. Some Critical and Nurturing Parent is a good thing, because it enables us to adopt standards and continuity, and to look after other people where we need to. We live with conventions and ways of doing things, and we do need some of that. Sometimes we need to make quick decisions, and don't have time to think things through with our Adult. If we had to think everything through this way, we would probably self-destruct!

Similarly, Adapted Child is no bad thing either. Whether we choose to comply or rebel, we are in some sense acknowledging that there is a set of rules in existence. There are conventions in place. We have also acknowledged that when using Adapted Child, the majority of us are more likely to comply with the dominant orthodoxy than to rebel against it. This has its uses too. With no Adapted Child, any rules would be potentially unenforceable – even if they were agreed democratically. Adapted Child does allow us to get on in the world, especially if we go along with the rules and conventions that are okay.

But what happens if they are not okay? Parent and Adapted Child on their own don't give us the tools either to realise this, or to do something about it. Those tools reside within the Adult and Free Child ego-states.

The System play

Our society's play then does not have much place for questioning and challenging on the one hand, or the spontaneous emotion and carefree behaviour on the other hand. This puts a rather restrictive straightjacket on us, adapting to authority, and being judgmental if at times nurturing of others. Our society is a 'parent – child' society, and in really big decisions we are the 'adapted children.'

Now this is all very well, but what are the consequences of this? Most of us end up being discouraged from bucking, ignoring, or actively questioning the system. Instead, we go along with the System as it is. In so doing, TA theory would suggest that we are taking away part of what makes us human.

This consequence may not seem all that important at first sight, but it is as we shall see. So why do we connive in the System game? The vast majority of us do connive in it, by choice or through unconscious ignorance. In the next chapter, we will begin to see just what happens when we interact with the authorities in our society, and the implications for us.

Chapter 6 – The systems weaknesses

- *Destiny is not a matter of chance; it is a matter of choice. It is not something to be waited for, but rather something to be achieved –* ***William Jennings Bryan***

The all-conquering Goliath

We have on the face of it an all-powerful, all-conquering economic Goliath that we can apparently do nothing about. An all – conquering Goliath that seems hell bent on consuming every resource worth having on this planet, and possibly removing all life from it in the end. Global warming and the near inevitable energy crisis are testimony to this – particularly with huge nations now entering the technology race. China, India, the Far East and South America are all building up a head of steam that is already challenging the traditionally dominant American and European powers, as well as competing for the same natural resources.

However, there is good news for us all. I believe we are capable of making the System change its game. The starting point for this belief of mine are two key weaknesses that are inherent in the System that so dominates our lives. The System may seem all powerful, but there are two things that it cannot stand. If we can find ways to 'get at' these weaknesses, the System will see it as a threat to the game that's being played. However, if we find the right way to do this, the System can do little about it, and will be forced to change in response. Oh, and guess what? I believe we can all do something about it. We can make Goliath reconsider his position!

What are these weaknesses then? The first is that the System inherently dislikes risk, uncertainty, and any behaviour it sees as irrational. Secondly, the System needs our attention, and it cannot stand it if we ignore it and take our attention somewhere else. Taking this to its conclusion, if enough of us start putting risk into the System, while ignoring it more often, and behaving irrationally a bit more, the System will have to change. That might sound like a bit much to believe at this stage, but it's time to find out.

Let's look in a little detail at each of these weaknesses – and the TA implications of each.

1. Dislike of risk and uncertainty

The System does not like risk and uncertainty, despite all the propaganda about entrepreneurship and taking risks. Political and business leaders may exhort the public to embrace change, yet the System itself doesn't like change, and cannot cope with a lot of it!

Let's consider the above statement in more detail.

The propaganda of risk

As we saw earlier, everyone who's anyone in our economic game talks about risk. Just consider these phrases – how many have you heard during your life?

- He (or she) who hesitates is lost.
- You have to speculate to accumulate.
- If you take the risk, you get the reward.

We reward risk-takers, and they are often idolised. Business leaders like Lord Alan Sugar, Sir Richard Branson and Duncan Bannatyne epitomise this mentality within Britain. They do so to the extent that they have become media personalities in their own right, often starring on TV shows. Similarly, in the US, risk takers like Steve Jobs and philanthropists like Bill Gates also stand out as household names.

These people may be popular, but they are not your normal business leaders. A second much larger category of business leaders are faceless wonders. I don't mean that in a derogatory sense, I just mean that you wouldn't know who they are. They are not leaders in any meaningful sense of the word, even if they are nominally in charge. They don't even take the risk of becoming known!

Of course, the media latch onto a third category of business leader, the ones who failed or did something spectacularly awful. To name a couple of them, Sir Fred Goodwin (ex-RBS) and John Browne (ex-BP), were brought down to earth spectacularly. Fred the Shred is the most vilified businessman of the last ten years in the UK. Stories now abound of his bullying tactics with staff, the size of his ego, and the fact that he was not a pleasant person. However, before his fall from grace with the collapse of RBS, Fred was feted by politicians, from UK Prime Ministers to Scottish First Ministers, who said nothing about his methods. He wasn't sacked from the System because he was a nasty man. He was sacked because he took a bad risk, and failed. His ego-fuelled takeover of the Dutch bank ABN Amro, stealing it from under the nose of Barclays amid a fanfare of idolisation, is now widely seen as the fatal move that left RBS high and dry when the banking sector hit difficulties. In short, Sir Fred lost his job because he got caught out taking a risk. Apparently, you are only allowed to take a risk if it is guaranteed to be a success. In my language, anything guaranteed to be a success isn't a risk in the first place.

Most corporations have risk management functions within them, with the brief that they are to manage risk in the organisation. Similarly, as any project manager will tell you (and I used to be one myself) an essential part of project and programme management lies in the management of risks. The language is important – for most situations, the "management of risks" effectively means the "minimisation of risks." Business and other organisations basically don't like the idea of risk. Even those speculating wildly on the stock market wouldn't do it if it was their own money they were speculating with. In practice, of course, it is other people's money! When you buy your own pension, you are often reassured (as I have been in the past) that "your risks are spread." In other words, they are hopefully minimised. So we ourselves reflect society's aversion to risk. The problem is, of course, that it's the businesses that minimise their risks by passing them on to us. Hence the phrase 'buyer beware.'

In financial services, you have no option but to 'buy.' You have no option but to place your money in a bank account, where who knows what happens to it? But for Government bail outs, we would have lost our money. The Northern Rock collapse in 2005 was accompanied by queues of people trying to withdraw their money from Northern Rock. But for Government intervention, there is no way they would have been successful. Similarly, we have little choice but to invest in a pension, little choice but to borrow to finance higher education (or if we are lucky enough, to save for it), and little choice but to take out a mortgage with a plethora of insurances that we just might need one day.

Look at how businesses react to the spectre of change, like a change of Government. They simply don't like the idea of change! The prospect of a radical change party winning any election is received with scepticism at best, and a run on the market at worst. At least part of the reason for this is that change marks new risk, and the System doesn't like that. Radicalism of the left or the right is often seen as threatening. Similarly the threat of countries declaring (or voting for) independence or withdrawing from Europe, is not seen as popular by business, who are generally anti-change.

In conclusion, businesses and government value consistency, reliability and predictability, whatever they may say to the rest of us. For our part, most people behave in a generally risk-averse way. We are often far too risk averse for our own good.

So what happens when we analyse this in TA terms? The whole idea behind risk is in doing something different. If we do what we did before, the outcome is more predictable. Doing what we did before is a quality of the Parent in us, if we are following previously recognised approaches. Alternatively, it can also be Adapted Child, if we are following the rules because otherwise we might get into trouble!

The System does not like unpredictability, even if it is the result of a well thought-through, Adult approach. Nor would it like the spontaneous approach of "go on, let's just do it." Yes, the Free Child is a big 'no-no', as far as the System is concerned. The irrational nature of Free Child is disliked by a System that does not like people doing irrational things. The dominant orthodoxy in modern life is that people should be rational, and our System prizes rational behaviour above all else. Economists repeatedly talk about the 'rational consumer.' (Do you remember the consumer word from before?) The word 'rational' does not mean 'Adult' in the TA sense of the word. Instead, it means 'behaving as we've been programmed.' As we have seen, being programmed means a combination of Adapted Child and Parent. We behave as we have been taught and learned to, rather than behaving in a particularly thought-driven way. 'Rational' carries with it the aura of predictability, and our society likes to predict what people are going to do. If we suddenly decided in large numbers to do something differently, that behaviour would be irrational, and the System would definitely not like it.

It is arguable that even opinion polls at election time have the bonus to the System of removing some of the unpredictability from what's likely to happen, and limit the choices the rest of us make. We are moved towards voting tactically for, or against, a party that might win.

Spontaneous, or otherwise different behaviour is discouraged as immature or not the accepted thing. If we're to be grown up, we really should be rational – and therefore risk averse. Using TA terms, the System does not welcome 'Free Child' behaviour, with any such behaviour often being derided as 'immature.' It would of course rather see Adapted Child behaviour, where we follow the rules.

It isn't just Free Child that gets it in the neck here. It is also our Adult ego-state that gets the boot. The System does not like divergent, different, articulated thought. This non-compliant thinking may prove to be a threat to it.

2. Loss of attention

The second thing that our System does not like is our taking our attention elsewhere. The System wants us to remain focused on it, and if we look elsewhere too much, it will try to find a way to regain our attention. The System acts a bit like a spoilt child, in that it wants our attention, and if necessary it will behave badly to get it! Behaving badly usually means creating some kind of crisis. It could be an economic crisis, a food crisis, a foreign crisis, or a war. In most western societies such crises are usually referred to as 'wars' anyway. I've lost track of how many literal and metaphorical wars we've had over the last ten years – wars on terror, bank wars, food wars, war on cattle disease, Ebola, and so on. Politicians and the media are good at whipping up a sense of crisis, often where there wasn't one before. Meanwhile, businesses use the same language to keep our attention – wars on the competition; new markets to fight for; if we don't change, we're finished, and so on.

Society is very good at maintaining our attention, through its cheerleaders of the media, politicians, and other actors on the stage. It is adept at keeping us in the game, generally with few exceptions – and many of those exceptions simply choose to drop out of society. There are significant numbers of people who reach a stage where they choose to 'go off and find themselves.' Some sort of world tour, or a visit to a remote part of the world, or even just heading off to a place of meditation. There are few examples of collective decisions to opt out, the most significant perhaps being the Hippie movement in the 1960's. But, over time, they gradually came back into the fold, and by the 1980's many of them were actively voting for right wing politicians or even occupying senior roles in businesses.

Of course, those who engage in outright rebellion are paying attention to society. Society does not mind this, as long as they don't go too far in their rebellious activities. If they do, they can always become one of the crises, or even become an excuse for a new war.

The irony is that the System, in getting our attention back, is doing so by almost behaving in an 'Adapted Child' way. If we take our attention elsewhere, the System's Adapted Child wants it back. But by creating a crisis to focus our attention, the System sparks our own Adapted Child back into action, as we compliantly turn our attention back to the game our System plays. Alternatively, we may respond to business leaders, politicians and the media by complaining, being critical or rebelling a bit. But all of these responses are either Adapted Child or Critical Parent in origin. They are not the responses of an Adult or Free Child. So, once again, we see what it is the System expects of us.

Society itself is an Adapted Child that chooses to exercise its Critical or Nurturing Parent on us if necessary to keep our attention on the game. This is done at all costs, in an attempt to provoke a response.

How can we spark change?

To many of us, the Goliath that is our economic and political system looks unassailable. It also behaves as if it is unassailable. However, that doesn't mean it cannot be changed – it can. Targeting the two areas we've just covered above provide the key to achieving some lasting change in our society and its dominant values. They represent the weak points in the game our society plays.

In other words, we need to learn to be more irrational, to take some risks, and to begin withdrawing our attention from the propaganda of the story our System chooses to tell us. Now this isn't easy, though it may be easier than we think. The key to making the System change is to focus on the TA ego states that are actively discouraged by our society; Adult and Free Child. Cultivating these parts of who we are will help to build a movement for change. We will see just how this happens in the next few chapters.

CREATE YOUR OWN REVOLUTION

We are at a point of opportunity, for both technological reasons, and because of the ongoing economic and environmental crises we now face. Starting to do some of these things that our system won't like will have one other side benefit, a significant side benefit. We will be getting a better handle on who we really are, and living a life that is more true to ourselves than the one that has been foisted on us by society. We will feel as if we are finally starting to live.

Part 2 - Creating the Solution

Chapter 7 - Regaining our lost talents

- *Nobody realises that some people expend tremendous amounts of energy merely to be normal -* ***Albert Camus***

So far in this book, we have diagnosed the issues with our current set up in society. I'm not going to re-cap on this, because it's too depressing! In some ways, the epidemics of stress, depression, alcoholism, substance abuse, obesity and self-harm say enough on their own about the mess we are in. We all know people who suffer from one or more of these illnesses. It's time to begin creating the solution. To this end, I have a confession to make. It's about my childhood, that time when we are learning to take our place in society. More importantly, it's also about the childhood of many other people I've met down the years.

I have some evidence for this because I have been a personal and career development consultant for many years now. After toying with the idea for the best part of a decade, I established my own business in 2009. As I started my own business up, I realised just what it was that I wanted my business to do. I wanted to help other people to rediscover their lost potential to be brilliant at something, because I believed that we all have the potential to be brilliant at something. We just need to find out what it is. That for me was a revelation, because for much of my life, I didn't believe I was brilliant at anything! Too many people believe this about themselves too.

I have two young children, whose role in life seems to be to constantly amaze me. They are talented, opinionated, creative, imaginative, and able to ask the most adult of questions – often the ones I don't want to answer! They can of course be exasperating at times, but that is just the other side of the coin. As I see my children getting older, I ask myself many different questions. How will they turn out? What sort of a life will they go on to lead? What will they look back on when they are my age? I imagine I share with all parents the hope that they will be looking back on a life of happiness, achievement and success.

I wonder what they will learn as they continue on their journey. What will happen to the talents they already possess in abundance? After all, as we go through life, its challenges and tribulations, we learn new skills, and how to adapt to get what we want or need. However, some of that adaptation involves unlearning things that we are born with, which are prominent during our early years.

As we grow up, most people to a greater or lesser extent lose three things they were born with. If we don't deal with these losses, we will be stunted for the rest of our life. The first thing we lose is the ability to be creative and playful. We cease these activities in the interests of 'growing up' and being serious. Secondly, we lose the belief that's it's okay to just be yourself, and that we are good enough as we are. Finally, we lose the ability to make ourselves heard, to express ourselves properly, becoming too concerned with saying the right thing, whatever that is.

Regaining at least some part of what we've lost to comply with the System's game matters if we are to regain our own self-identity of who we are. If you're sitting there thinking you've lost yourself, or your life, then it's likely that your losses are in the areas we've just talked about. But regaining these qualities is also the key to igniting change for the better in our society. As the great Indian independence leader Mohandas Gandhi said all those years ago, we should 'be the change we want to see in the world.' By regaining our lost qualities and applying them, we can indeed change the world. Before we do that, let's look in a bit more detail at these qualities we have lost, along with some ideas on how it is we unlearn them.

The first loss - being creative

Children are born creative. As anyone who has young children will know, they have great ability to be both creative and playful. My two young children have the following talents in bucket-loads. They both have vivid imaginations. They are not afraid to try to paint, draw or crayon pictures, often on unsuitable surfaces (like the dining room table!) They both play without a care in the world, totally engrossed in whatever it is they are doing. They are not afraid to try different things, just to see what would happen. Children also create plays, as in playing houses or pretending they are invisible. Unlike us adults, they aren't bothered about taking a creative risk or two, and getting disapproval from others, or being seen as silly. Didn't we all use our imaginations when we were younger? I bet you can recall vividly when you did use your imagination.

The sad thing is that we often lose our creative imagination as we 'grow up'. We learn lessons like "imagination is not real", or "painting won't get you a job", and we are disciplined out of being creative. We are encouraged to dress to conformity, particularly in schools – and the pressures to conform come at an early age. Boys wear blue and girls wear pink. As Sir Ken Robinson's brilliant speech a few years ago made plain, our education systems are geared to developing left brain activities, like analysis, arithmetic and the sciences, at the expense of right brain creative activities, like music, dance, the arts and generally just being imaginative and creative. (1)

Not only does this strategy kill half our brain, it also costs society dear. How many great strides forward have been made as the result of great analysis alone? The answer is 'not a lot'. From the first man on the moon to Einstein's theory of relativity, even the great scientific and engineering feats have come about as the result of creative imagination.

The Biblical reference to 'putting away childish things' as we grow up is reflected in some of the more strict Christian sects who seem to be taught that, whatever they do in life, followers should under no circumstances have any fun! I'm not making a religious point here so much as just emphasising the fact that, as adults, we are supposed to engage in rational behaviour. This eliminates the need for us to be creative, or have fun. In fact, those who remain that way are often viewed as immature or unreliable. Unreliable for the System, that is!

To use the terms in Transactional Analysis, we are being invited to put our Free Child into the bin, lock the lid, and throw away the key. Part of our humanity is stunted or disappears as we grow up. Later on, often in our teenage years, we may learn a different way to be creative. This involves following different fashions, and creating a self-image. It might include graffiti on walls, acting, or dressing outlandishly. But this 'creativity' is different from before. It is not Free Child. Instead, it is Adapted Child. We are learning either to comply with or rebel against the dominant fashions. To give just one example, someone in my childhood who was a punk and followed the music is likely to have been doing it for one of two reasons. Either they were complying with their mates who had become punks, or they were rebelling against society and their parents. Neither of these is a Free

Child stance, and had I pointed this out to them at the time, they would probably have killed me!

Our playful, creative, imaginative nature isn't the only part of us that is lost on this journey to adulthood, and to playing the System game. We also have other baggage to ditch on route to becoming a partial human being.

The second loss - being yourself

Isn't it amazing how babies and children have no problem with being themselves? They hold no sense of social inadequacy, that they are not worthy of attention. They have no problem with thinking they are worth it. They do not hide parts of themselves they don't want others to see. They don't hold back from projecting their personality, warts and all. They don't disguise their intentions. In other words, babies and young children are born authentic, and they behave in a way that is true to who and what they are. They say what they stand for, and lack that sense of shame. We are born authentic.

Then we lose it.

As we grow up, we learn to put on different acts for the benefit of different people. We are told what it's acceptable to do, and not do. Parts of our character are corrected by those in authority in our lives. We learn a sense of shame for aspects of who we are; we might have a quick temper, or we may say 'I want' too often. We might want to keep ourselves to ourselves sometimes, or chatter on endlessly. We learn to adapt, to hide bits of ourselves, and generally to disguise what we want, how we feel, what we think, and who we are. We learn to do what everyone else does, for fear of standing out from the crowd. Standing out risks being ridiculed, which is unpleasant. If we have a view we think is unpopular, we hold it in just in case others find it disagreeable or worse. We don't ask a question in case we're seen as stupid for asking it in the first place. So we lose that childhood ability to question things to satisfy our curiosity.

We might pretend that we like a job, or like a person, when we don't like it or them at all. We accumulate a range of negative beliefs and self doubts as we grow up that prevent us from being ourselves.

Now I want you to forget about society for a moment. This unwillingness to show our true self happens in comparatively trivial situations sometimes. Remember those office Christmas parties where family members are also invited? How comfortable is that, for your work colleagues to meet your spouse and family? I reckon part of the reason for discomfort is that many people behave completely differently at work, from with their family, and that makes it hard to work out how you're going to behave on THAT night. "Oh, I hope he doesn't get talking to her!" We have learned to put on a false face, and not be ourselves, and we risk this act being exposed when two worlds meet.

'Being ourselves' sounds so easy in principle, but for many people it feels both unattainable, and painful – facing up squarely to our own lack of self worth. However, this lack of self worth we feel has largely been foisted on us by guess what? The System!

That's the reason why authentic leadership is all the rage in organisational life at the moment. It's all the rage because so many people are not authentic. We cover up our own shame often by finding others to blame or criticise. Authenticity is a fad that isn't happening because the dominant ethos in our society is against this. The emphasis on Parent and Adapted Child behaviour at the expense of Adult and Free Child makes it hard for most people to be authentic – particularly when the dominant Adapted Child strategy most of us use is to comply with authority.

In TA terms, we develop our Critical Parent, by self-criticising or criticising other people, measuring them up against a set of standards. We also learn to adapt our behaviour to what we think those in authority want. In other words, we boost our Adapted Child. We sacrifice our Adult, the ability to think and express ourselves independently.

The third loss - being heard

Babies are born with terrific power. They aren't afraid to express their needs. Okay, they are pretty basic needs, but babies and toddlers know how to turn up the volume. They are so much louder than adults. They haven't yet learned how to mumble! They aren't afraid to ask – or demand – things. Children are good at expressing their wants in a way that is heard.

Has it ever struck you as odd that, as we get bigger, we also become quieter? As we grow up, we lose the voice we started out with. It's rude to ask or demand. We're told to be quiet. We learn to lose our power under pressure from society, schools and parents, not to mention from other people of our age. Isn't it ironic that babies are on the face of it powerless, yet they know how to be powerful? Adults, by contrast, are much more powerful, yet so many of us lose our voice by the time we reach this stage. In a manner of speaking, we throw out the baby with the bath-water. While there is a need to use our voice more intelligently, and in a more socially skilled way as we grow older, many of us lose it completely. We dampen our light and settle for less than we might have. The other element in this loss is that we hold back from asserting ourselves in the first place. Perhaps we fear our own power as human beings. Maybe that's no surprise given that the word 'power' has such a negative connotation anyway. Power tends to be abused, and as Lord Acton pointed out many years ago, 'absolute power is abused absolutely.'

As we grow up then, we suppress our own volume and personal power, and become much less than we could have been.

What can TA tell us about this loss? Much of this loss of voice is down to not expressing our views, wants or opinions at the time. Part of the problem is not formulating and then articulating a thought through view, which would be the Adult ego state. The other part we often lose is the spontaneity to "say it as we see it", and this spontaneity comes from Free Child. The smaller, shriller voice we end up with is a combination of Adapted Child, where we go along with or less commonly rebel against the dominant view expressed elsewhere, or we adopt the blame game epitomised by Critical Parent. In extreme form, this leads us to spend most of our time finding people to blame for what is wrong!

This has been epitomised recently in the Scottish Independence Referendum, when the public and media criticised politicians on both sides of the debate for their failure to provide relevant facts so the electorate could make up its mind. Now, it was true that politicians were not stepping forward to answer a number of key questions that would help people decide which way to vote. However, behind this request for clarity, I reckon many members of the electorate wanted the facts dished up to them conveniently, like a children's meal at 5.30pm, so they wouldn't need to do any real thinking themselves. There is no such set of facts that can do this. But clearly the thought of having to think the issues through for themselves (Adult), and to perhaps even make the decision partially on emotional attachment (independence for Scotland, or the Union?) proved to be a challenge for much of the electorate. Of course, the emotional bit would be Free Child.

So it is that the Critical Parent – Adapted Child game goes on, at the same time as we lose much of our humanity.

*****

There you have it. As adults, we lose much of our creative, fun side, along with our own sense of self-worth and with it our desire to be ourselves, and finally our ability to make ourselves heard to other people. It's no wonder that so many people live lives of quiet desperation. It's also no wonder that our society motors on regardless, and continues to play its part in stunting the development of the next generation. In particular, as we see, the talents and qualities emanating from our Adult and Free Child ego states are actively discouraged in the dominant System game we're expected to play.

Our loss to society

As we mature, most of us learn to project the things that society values. Essentially this means we learn to behave more in line with our Adapted Child, allied with both Critical and Nurturing Parent. The Parent ego state comes in usually when we see other people not complying with the requirements of authority, at whatever level it operates. There is a more positive Parent role of course, which is to help those who might need it.

Both variations of Adapted Child are entirely acceptable as far as the System is concerned. The compliant Adapted Child is what the System requires from the majority. It needs us to show willingness to go along with the dominant orthodoxy, in a relatively unquestioning way. Luckily, we human beings are programmed from a very early age to go along with things. That's how fashions work. However, the rebellious version of Adapted Child is also welcome to some degree. Our System of society needs some people to rebel, to push back on it. Society gains strength from having a level of protest. It gives our politicians and media something to focus on, and often it gives society the enemy it needs to fight as a way of keeping our attention on the game. As we saw earlier, this notion of Society having an enemy designed to keep the population's attention on the game rather than on what's really going on was brilliantly depicted by George Orwell in his futuristic novel *1984*. (It was, of course, futuristic when it was written in 1948!)

So if we over-emphasise two aspects of who we are, what do we lose? It's obvious from what we've talked about already. We lose the Free Child part of us. We lose the ability to be creatively spontaneous, to be free of constraints, the ability to play and have fun. There are millions of grown-ups in our society who look like they have none of these things in their lives. For them, fun was abolished at the age of 18, or perhaps even earlier. We also lose the Adult ego-state, to some extent. We lose the ability to think originally, and for ourselves. Instead, we re-think thoughts that have been programmed into us by other people. With this loss of Adult, we stop critically examining what's going on around us, and simply accept it. What "thinking" we do comes from either Critical Parent, or Adapted Child. We end up rationalising to ourselves why we went along with the majority view, or with what the 'authorities' told us.

Comedians are interesting people, not just because they make us laugh. It often takes a comedian to point out the absurdity of modern life, by examining day-to-day life from different angles. As a result of their descriptions, we laugh at the absurdity. Comedians use their Adult faculty to give us a good laugh, and unleash our Free Child. It's no wonder we leave the show, or switch the TV off feeling better as the result of watching them. Comedy is one of the ways we rebalance some of what goes on in our lives. What a shame we don't re-balance the rest of our lives as well. We would feel so much better! This might also help explain why so many comedians end up becoming more politically active later on – like Tony Robinson and Elaine C Smith, for example.

So we link back from ourselves and how we feel, to our society and how it is under the dominant System game we play. The key to changing our society for the better is to use our Adult and Free Child to spark change by highlighting the absurdity of it all, and then to literally choose to play a different game. The System won't like that one bit, but if we do it in the right spirit, it will have no choice but to change in response. Like a stroppy child, if its tactics aren't working, it will need to do something different. And that, my friends, is what we all want.

What our sick society needs is more of the natural talents we lose as we grow up. More of those talents that we lose as we take our place in society with all the pressures that exist there. Being creative, being yourself and being heard are the keys that will transform the place we live in.

But how do I do this? How do I re-learn what I've unlearned? It is to this place that we now go.

Chapter 8 – The opportunity to change

- *Too many people are thinking of security rather than opportunity. They seem more afraid of life than death – **James F Bynes***

If you have read this far, you are probably convinced of the need to change. It's either that, or you are looking to pick holes in my arguments! Seriously though, one question you may be holding onto is "how do we convince the majority to do something to change the game that has put us in the mess we're in?" The assumption, of course, is that we do need a majority to get something done, something that radical movements in the past have failed to achieve. Or so we think.

I'm going to start with a history lesson, one I've been reading about recently. Let's look at where sustainable change can happen, and why it does. What lessons can we learn from this, compared to movements for change that ultimately failed to achieve anything?

Generating change – the American Civil Rights movement

It is over fifty years ago that the Reverend Martin Luther King Junior stood up in front of the Washington memorial, at the largest civil rights protest in American history, and made his now iconic "I have a dream" speech. Many black leaders from all walks of American life attribute much of the progress achieved in the USA on civil rights to that march, the movement that organised the march, and moved on after it.

It is an extraordinary achievement given the situation that black people suffered under in 1963. The Southern states were shamefully segregated, in a way that wasn't that different from Apartheid inspired South Africa in the 1960's. Blacks were not allowed into 'responsible' jobs, they went to inferior schools, they were viewed by many whites as being little better than apes. They were also denied the vote along with many other civil rights the rest of the population took for granted. They also constituted a minority group within the USA.

In short, they were a minority in a seriously disadvantaged position. How on earth were they able to succeed?

Part of the reason was simply that they were determined. Inspired by Martin Luther King's advocacy of non-violent protest, they engaged with significant sections of the white community. The spectre of non-violent protest in southern cities like Birmingham being met by police brutality also appalled many Americans who wondered if this was the kind of society their Founding Fathers had wanted when they issued the American Declaration of Independence. This in turn led to significant numbers of whites flocking to the banner of equality and justice. So it is that we fast forward to today, with people like Barack Obama and Oprah Winfrey making clear that they owe it all to those actions of 50 years ago. Like Nelson Mandela did many years later in South Africa, King was able to embrace his captors, while disagreeing with what they were doing.

As a result, while there is much that could be better in race relations attitudes within the USA, the progress made since those dark days in 1963 has been little short of astounding. In some ways, a similar story could be told about race relations in Britain. I'm going to tell that story too as an illustration on why things change.

Generating change - Race relations in Britain

In the 1980's, at the height of the Margaret Thatcher era, Britain's race relations record was pretty shameful. We had the scene of Stop and Search (SUS) police powers in London, often misused against the West Indian community. We heard racist whites complaining about lazy West Indians coming here and taking our benefits while not working, while simultaneously complaining about workaholic Asian Indians and Pakistanis coming here, working long hours, and taking our jobs away. Immigrants were damned if they worked and damned if they didn't. In some ways we could argue that not much has changed – in 2015, we hear complaints about Poles, Rumanians and other East Europeans which sound remarkably similar, and just as racist.

But let's turn back to the original Commonwealth immigrants. While it's not nirvana out there nowadays, there is little doubt that these groups are much more integrated into mainstream Britain than before – to the extent that not that long ago, I heard a British citizen of West Indian descent berating the recent East European immigrants as not being 'English.' Oh yes, second and third generation Commonwealth immigrants are now so integrated that they've taken on our bad habits!

How did this improvement happen for our Commonwealth influx? It wasn't the result of anything our politicians did. If anything, they got in the way of progress. Nor was it the result of particularly enlightened policing, as recent scandals in the Metropolitan Police continue to demonstrate. It is simply down to people getting to know people, and finding out that they're not that different to us. It's easy to be racist if we clump groups of people together in ignorance to say "they're all like that." It becomes more difficult when our children go to school with them, their best friend is an immigrant, or when we start working next to people who moved in from abroad. Nothing breaks down barriers faster than simply getting to know people. The racist views of a generation ago are anathema to the current generation, who mixed more readily, and even by their mid-twenties have met more nationalities than their parents ever did.

People trust those they see and like. That basic approach meant two small minorities successfully sparked change in two western societies. Understanding this point is one key to how we can now spark meaningful social and political change in the modern era in Britain and beyond. So how many people would it take to do this? The answer is perhaps not as many as you think. As it was in the case of US and UK race relations, so it can be for wider change in society. It won't be a majority that are needed to spark change in our System.

Let's look at this with another example of how change sparked by a minority of people took hold and forced change not only on one country, but in an entire region of the world.

The 2011 Arab Spring

The Arab Spring began in Tunisia, in December 2010, when a Tunisian market stall seller refused to pay market bribes, and had his goods confiscated. After appealing to the authorities for his goods to be returned, he set himself on fire – injuries from which he eventually died. It is hard to understand what would drive anyone to do this, but in many ways it's what happened next that was most important. On hearing this news, angry crowds came onto the streets of Sidi Bouzid, a provincial city in Tunisia. Crowds also flooded onto the streets of other Tunisian cities and towns. Despite the violent start, these demonstrations were largely peaceful, and positive in intent. By mid-January

2011, the President had resigned, ushering in significant change, and the democratisation of Tunisia.

But this was not the end. By February 2011, two months after the initial trigger in Tunisia, mass protests had spread to Algeria, Libya, Egypt, Jordan, Palestine, Yemen and Morocco. Nor did it end there – and it didn't always lead to great results either. But the main point is made.

Essentially, this all began when a few Arabs decided to do something inconvenient. It wasn't a convenient thing to do to protest. In the face of authoritarian and dictatorial regimes, it was actually dangerous. But at the start, the protestors did something different from normal, even though they were small in number.

Doing nothing would have meant the Egyptian dictator Hosni Mubarak would still be in charge of the country, with his Police State in tow. Instead, a few people decided to do something inconvenient. Rather than take the convenient option, which is always to do nothing, they elected to do something, to make an uncomfortable stand. As more and more people decided to do something personally inconvenient, change started to happen right in front of their eyes (and our TV eyes). The use of social networking sites like Facebook and Twitter spread the word.

That is the point. If we want something to change, it will only ever happen if we choose to do something inconvenient. To make a stand on something, at whatever level that stand needs to take place. It means attempting to behave in a different, uncomfortable way. To challenge our own thinking even if it's what we've always believed. The pursuit of inconvenience is one of the keys to sparking change.

The Arab Spring led to some positive change, but also setbacks in other countries, and at its worst, war and carnage. However, let's now turn our attention to a completely different type of movement that ultimately failed in its attempt to ignite change in society, despite its great intentions at the time. It goes back to the era of the Beatles and Vietnam.

Failing to generate change – the Hippie movement

In the 1960's, we saw the rise in the Western world of what became known as the Hippie movement. This movement comprised many different aspects, from love and peace to sex, drugs, flowers, and rock and roll. It provided a counter-culture to the dominant western orthodoxy, providing both an alternative lifestyle, and opposition to the Vietnam War, and anti-nuclear protest. At the time, it looked like it could change the world. Yet it failed to achieve this change, even if it did influence at least some of what happened afterwards. Many of those active in this movement in the late sixties became the conventional money makers under the auspices of President Reagan and Margaret Thatcher in the 1980's.

It is clear that many in this movement sought an alternative, sought meaning in life - even if they had colourful ways of finding it! It's also clear that the media and dominant society criticised them, perhaps not without some merit. Dirty, drug-fuelled, sex obsessed, drop-outs became the enemy for senior politicians and media, in the same way as North Vietnam was for the military leadership. Some of the Hippie phenomenon was a reaction to the dominant focus on conventional materialism and affluence, which they saw as inauthentic - again, not without reason. One article of the time described the Hippie code as "Do your own thing, wherever you have to do it and whenever you want. Drop out. Leave society as you have known it. Leave it utterly. Blow the mind of every straight person you can reach. Turn them on, if not to drugs, then to beauty, love, honesty, fun." (1)

These words say it all. 'Do your own thing', 'drop out', and 'fun' all speak of the Free Child within us. It is less clear how much 'Adult' is in there. But it is clearly a reaction to the dominant mores of society, which was – and is – Critical Parent and Adapted Child in nature. However, there are other words in there. Consider 'drop out' and 'leave it utterly.' They are words that symbolise dropping out completely from society and having nothing more to do with it.

There are many reasons why this movement under-achieved, and in my view the main one is that they largely opted out of society. They chose not to engage with it. While they may have chosen to play a different game, they weren't in a position to influence other people. It's hard to influence other people if you don't engage with them. As we have seen, people buy things, ideas and approaches from people who they like, know and trust. That can't happen if those playing a different game are sitting in a commune somewhere.

The desire for communal life may have been understandable to a hippy, but it was a fatal mistake to the hope of changing anything much. We may want to play a different game, but we must remain on the same stage so people can see us. By not staying on the same stage, the Hippies allowed the media and politicians to tell us all how awful the play was, and put everyone else off knowing anything about them. So the Critical Parent – Adapted Child game continued in their absence. You cannot change something by simply removing yourself from it. We need to change the game, but stay on the stage!

Then other people can make their choice at first hand.

Igniting social change

"Never doubt that a small group of thoughtful, committed citizens can change the world; Indeed, It's the only thing that ever has." - Margaret Mead

So how small a number are we talking about? One thing is clear - it certainly doesn't need to be anywhere near 50%. Human beings have a high propensity to follow ideas, fads and fashions. That's how the System managed to get its hold on us in the first place. However, that means we can use this fact to our advantage. After all, no fashion sets out with universal appeal at the start. Any fashion begins with a few people; then it becomes a trend, and the rest is history. So how many people would it take to start something special? I will return to the 'how many' question very shortly.

I believe we can learn from the changes talked about above to work out what needs to happen. We will start igniting significant change when enough people know someone who is doing something different. Change will happen when we get to the point where most people know someone who has started to play a different game from the System one. Be it a friend, relative, or work colleague, we notice someone who is doing something different. My answer begs two further questions. They are both big questions, and I will answer them in the rest of this book.

- Question 1 – What is the different thing that we need to do?
- Question 2 – How do we ensure that other people find out about it, so they get to know someone who is doing something different?

Returning to the numbers question for the moment, there is a law of networking called the law of 250. (2) You may have heard of it? I refer to this 'law' in my career coaching, when I am helping people to find a job they want. This law states that the average person knows up to 250 people. That doesn't necessarily mean you know them well, but you know them well enough to recognise them and you know something about each other. This is an average, so you may know fewer, or more, than 250 other people.

How many of these people would need to be doing something different before you would take notice of them? Would you start to notice if 10 people you knew started doing something different? What about if it was 25 people? I think most people would notice if 10% of the people they knew started doing something differently. We can see this on a trivial level at times. Just look at the recent explosion in taking 'selfies' where you take a picture of yourself using your mobile phone, in front of something famous, or with someone famous. That trend began with a few people, and caught on to the point that even members of the British Royal Family have done it. The proliferation of 'selfies' was helped no end by social networking sites, where the photos were posted for others to see. More recently even than this has been the trend of arranging to have ice-cold water poured over yourself, and videoing the event, so you can post it online and nominate three more people to do it. This fashion engulfed Facebook and Twitter during the summer of 2014, and raised significant sums of money for charity. Again, what began as a small idea mushroomed into a major media talking point. It also arguably did some good. How much more effective would it be if we could harness social networking to engage people to ignite change in our System?

The message from all this is clear. Once everyone knows someone who plays a different game, we are into change territory. Especially if those people look to us like they are enjoying playing a different game from the stifling one that is our current society. Just 10% of the population would very likely be a critical mass for this to happen. 10% is enough for everyone to know someone significant to them who is doing things differently. 10% of people turning their attention away from society and playing a different game is enough to spark a reaction from the dominant forces in our society. 10% of the population choosing to play to hope rather than succumb to the fear that drives our society could have a massive impact.

Any good sales theory will tell you that people buy from those they trust. They buy when they see something better than what they have, and want some of it. That goes for ideas as well as products. People buy ideas from those they like and trust; those who are like them. If they see a better idea, they will move to it. Now the great thing about playing a different game is that, as we will see, it involves coming alive. It means really choosing to live, not just exist. Being alive has its own attraction, its own shelf-life, and other people who don't have it will want some of it. Playing to hope and aspiration rather than fear and despair will attract other people to be around you, and want to be like you.

It's no surprise that you would feel more alive. After all, the antidote to the System game involves re-connecting with the parts of us that are Adult and Free Child. Fun goes with that territory. Fresh, real thinking goes with that territory. Living goes with that territory, and most people will readily buy that kind of life if they see they could have it!

The unique opportunity – why now?

We may think of ourselves as individuals, and indeed we are. But we also have a herding instinct. As part of this, we imitate what we see, especially if we like it. But how do we create that 'herd' instinct when our communities have to a great extent broken down? It was in the late 1980's that UK Prime Minister Margaret Thatcher boasted words to the effect that "there is no such thing as society." As we will see, you don't even need to leave your town or home to start creating some sense of community, and movement for change.

There are two reasons why I believe now might be the right time – the opportunity to communicate online through internet and social media, and secondly the near total disdain in which the authorities are now held by members of the public.

Reason 1: The opportunity to communicate on the internet and social media

The first reason why now might be the right time is the advent of the internet and social media. This has created an opportunity to communicate with others that was not open to us before. We are now able to talk to people from across the planet, to connect with other people who have similar interests to ourselves. It's an opportunity that the dominant powers in our society are trying to control, but not entirely successfully. Facebook, Twitter and YouTube among other sites have given us all the chance to communicate just what's going on in our lives. Even Wikipedia has allowed us to share information that was previously inaccessible. We are able to do our own research on a subject should we wish to, more easily than ever before.

We don't need to look far to see the impact of social media. Just cast your mind back to 2011, and the impact of YouTube and Facebook in driving protest in countries like Tunisia and Egypt at the start of the Arab Spring. They provided a springboard for change, with oppressive Governments toppling as a result of action taken by ordinary people.

Terrorist cells across the world have mastered the ability to use social networking as a way to communicate plans. If those intent on death and destruction can do this, why not the rest of us? Social networking gives us opportunity to at least build a community of thought, translating into a community of action.

It is indeed ironic how so much of the antidote to the dominant System has already been sussed out by those seeking to destroy it, using terrifying means to do so. We have seen it in the murderous attacks on the twin towers, to city centre rioters, to jihadists and beheadings. Those who don't care much for ethics and morality and are hell-bent on destruction have realised the weak points of the System, and are prepared to act against it. They also realise the opportunity presented by new technologies to develop large, passionate followings in support of change. They have grabbed the opportunity to create a different type of organisation. A cell is now simply a different type of organisation. Thirty years ago, a cell was where you went if you broke the law.

Riots and terror attacks are organised on Facebook and Twitter, ransom requests on YouTube, and attention is being diverted from the dominant game.

They have cashed in on the System's dislike of risk and uncertainty. Apart from being evil in intent, they have certainly behaved in a way that seems openly irrational. Finally, they have successfully diverted attention away from the game, at least to a degree. However, the game they choose to play is a hellish alternative version. Instead of relatively benign suppression of people, their hopes and values as at present, many of these groups would replace that with prejudice, murder, torture and mayhem.

The fact that in some cases relatively well educated people have signed up with this is a warning though. The System is rotten, and we need a different game. The irony is that, if we want to change things, we need to learn in some cases from what the terrorists themselves do, and stop being so compliant.

Reason 2 - Mistrust of the 'authorities'

The second reason why now might be the right time to act is the fallout from years of austerity, accompanied by record levels of stress and depression existing in our society. We've seen increased environmental protest against everything from fracking to oil exploitation in the developing world. G7, G8 and G15 summits (how many G's are there?) are accompanied by protest and sometimes violence. I know of one chef in Wales who underwent months of vetting procedures because she worked at a hotel that was hosting a NATO summit in 2014. Otherwise, no-one would be bothering her. We see increased concern for the future of our planet, with climate change now a generally accepted fact.

We now see near-to-universal disdain at the 'authorities' who have spent the last decade telling the rest of us to tighten our belts. Governments, be they at Westminster, Capitol Hill or Brussels are often held in near-contempt by the public. Confidence in the integrity and competence of our public institutions has never been at such a low point. In Scotland, it was clear that a key part of the 'Yes' campaign in the Scottish independence referendum was not so much nationalist as simply a desire to get away from Westminster rule, and all the arrogance and corruption that has gone with that. That discontent nearly resulted in the end of a 300-year old Union between countries.

Such discontent is not confined to Scotland however. The recent European elections produced a combination of low turnouts and high votes for protest parties. The one thing they all had in common was a discontent with the way Europe operates. This discontent can be no surprise given the treatment of the Mediterranean countries on austerity, and the way that previous referenda on European issues have been repeatedly ignored by the Central European powers. Countries like Ireland (twice) and Denmark have been sent away to think and vote again after initial referenda that said no to European integration in different areas. Like naughty children they were sent away, and like Adapted Children, they complied and voted the right way the second time.

*****

Social media plus the fallout from what is close to a decade of austerity and the discontent generated by our system of Government makes now a unique opportunity to change the game we play, and to spark change in our society as a result. Indeed, now must be the right time to change. As Martin Luther

CREATE YOUR OWN REVOLUTION

King Junior said, "the time is always right to do what is right." So what do we do?

What if we simply play a different game, rather than rebel against the dominant game? What if we disengage rather than rebel? What if we choose not to fight an 'enemy' or even see one? Our System needs people to fight it, but what if we don't do this? We don't need to rebel against anything if we choose not to see an enemy.

I mentioned the three talents earlier on, talents which most of us lose to a greater or lesser extent. It is time to rediscover them. In doing so, we will divert our own and other people's attention from the dominant game our System plays. In doing this, we will – to use the metaphor of that famous children's tale – expose the emperor as having no clothes. If we start doing things differently, other people will follow; humans like to follow people they like to do things they like the look of. The first part of ourselves we need to rediscover is our playful, creative potential. It is the part of us that will try something "just to see what happens." We need to reconnect with the Free Child in us.

Chapter 9 – Regain our playful, creative side

- *We don't stop playing because we grow old. We grow old because we stop playing – **George Bernard Shaw***

This is the first step to creating your own revolution. We are all born playful and creative. We are born with a vibrant Free Child, the side of us that is curious and wants to learn things for their own sake. Asking 'why' all the time is about finding out why things work the way they do, and how they work. However, not only are the answers provided often not satisfying ('because I say so'), but society has a more insidious way of dealing with this question. Society discourages us from asking it in the first place!

A sense of humour and fun also fit into the Free Child approach. It is perhaps no surprise that the most trenchant criticism of the way our society works comes from comedians, a point alluded to in chapter seven. Comedians use humour to make a point, and make us all realise how absurd the society is that we live in. Unfortunately, when we leave the performance or switch the TV off, we simultaneously put our Free Child back in its box. After all, we've all had a laugh. But it's now time to be grown up again.

Do you recognise any of these thoughts in your children – or in yourself if you can remember back far enough?

- "Let's pull this plug out, just to see what happens"
- "Let's see how far I can push mummy before she snaps!"
- "What if I cycle through the flower bed?"
- "I've been told I can't do this, so I will!"

Children like to try out small things, to push the boundaries out and see what they can do. They try things just to see what will happen. They challenge or disregard authority, actively testing the environment they are in. Alas, for most of us, this faculty is blunted to our loss in later life.

So, how do I let my Free Child out to play? Here are some ideas on how you can start to do this. Bear in mind though that Free Child is spontaneous and creative, so you might find other ways to let it out.

Start small

If you've gone half your life never doing anything creative or playful, don't overdo it at first. Start on the small stuff, but try something "just to see what happens." You can try something bigger next time around. Just find ways to let your natural, curious child out. Start playing around with the authorities, just to see what they do.

Let' say your bank has annoyed you in some way. Phone or send them an email saying you plan to close your account, even if in practice you have no intention of doing so! Let's just see what happens. You're fed up wearing conventional clothing at the office to comply with their office-wear policy? Then wear something different – a yellow tie, or something that's just a little bit tatty, just for the hell of it. Alternatively, go for a brown trouser day, do something completely cool or un-cool. Doing small things first will get you more used to letting your Free Child out to play. The important point here is to find creative ways to play around. There will be bigger things you can do later, believe me.

Make it communal

To add to the fun, turn this first step into a more communal activity. The key to making it communal is to tell your friends, neighbours, and internet contacts what you're doing. People are herd animals, and may well join in. Imagine the fun if your brown trouser, tatty t-shirt or yellow tie catches on, and other people start impersonating what you do, or try out something different of their own. In a small way, you and they will be starting to play a different game. How would the boss react if half their team followed an un-cool fashion, just for one day?

We also need to communicate because once we start to play a different game on more significant issues, we will want to use our communication channels for bigger things. Tell your friends and colleagues about what you're up to.

Play where you want to

You don't have to be overly influenced by other people in deciding what you want to do. We are all unique people, and our Free Child might not choose to focus on the same things as other people would. Do something different that is you. Whether it's not paying for something because the service is poor, or promising to close an account, whatever it is. Find a way to express yourself.

For example, I know someone who, when faced with a credit card bill he couldn't pay, sent the company a picture of a smiley face he had drawn. When the company phoned him to chase payment up (and to check he was sane) he explained that he was an artist, and his picture was worth the same amount as the credit card bill. Of course, he ended up paying the bill, but he had some fun in the process. More significantly, for our purposes, the company did not know how to handle this outburst of irrational behaviour!

As another example, I participated in the 2014 European elections. My view at the time was that it was pretty futile voting for any of the political parties that were standing for election. None of them appeared to be listening to voters, the European Parliament is a rubber stamp, while the powers that be within the European Union were not showing any interest in listening to public opinion.

I could have done what the majority of eligible voters chose to do – not bother to vote. However, I elected (sorry about the pun!) to express my feelings, and chose a fun way to do it. So I turned up to the polling station with a set of coloured pens, and did what any Free Child would do. I spoiled my ballot paper, but did so creatively. As someone who was told at School that he was no good at art, I drew a (very bad) picture, and wrote a speech outlining why I wasn't voting. I also ventured one or two mischievous comments about some of the candidates. I spent 15 minutes doing this, despite realising that the eyes of the polling station staff were on me. I then probably broke the law by taking a photo of the ballot paper, before putting it in the box, and leaving. I also posted this picture on Facebook, which sparked some interesting conversation about why I had done it. In short I made a point, misbehaved, and had some fun. That is not a bad combination! No doubt I gave one of the election counters a bit of a laugh too.

This example gives a great microcosm of how our society really works. In that Polling Station, there is no privacy. I was always being observed.

Other voters could not see what I was doing, but the staff could see everything. The voting table is also at the wrong height to do much more than put an 'x' in the box with a pencil. I had to stoop to draw anything. It's a good job that I don't suffer from a bad back!

Isn't it interesting too to see the language that society uses to describe what I did that day? I 'spoiled' my ballot paper. Like a bad boy, I ruined it! I didn't comply with the rules that say I should be a good person and follow the rules. I didn't think I spoiled my ballot paper. Instead, I enhanced its quality significantly, even given my limited artistic powers! What was also interesting was when I read an article afterwards on the BBC website making clear that any voters taking a photo of themselves voting risked being prosecuted, and that polling station staff should keep a look out for this. Apparently, it is illegal to accidently disclose your own ballot paper number by photographing it. Taking a selfie (or self-portrait) also risks having someone else in the background, who is voting, and that is also illegal.

One important point to make about these 'childish' protests is that they should not be motivated by malice or anger. If they are so motivated, then we are succumbing to the Critical Parent / Adapted Child behaviour our society values so much. In Critical Parent mode, we are angry at their (bad) behaviour, and we want to make a point. Alternatively, we are being the Adapted Child our society also values, and choosing this time to rebel against the System. This might make us feel better in some way, but we are still playing the same game as society is. We are deferring to the dominant System. With Free Child, we are doing it much more "just to see what happens." We are giving the message that we are no longer taking responsibility for playing the futile game we are currently part of.

The message from this step is clear. Do it lightly, do it with fun. But, in the words of Nike, just do it.

Why this matters

All this matters because you are starting to push out the boundaries from what you've done since you grew up. It also matters because the System we are so fed up with won't like it very much. Like a child with a parent, we are looking to try out different things, just to see what will happen. The system will struggle to comprehend or cope with such random, "immature" behaviour.

CREATE YOUR OWN REVOLUTION

The aim of this step is the same as it is with a young child. We are testing the boundaries of what we can reasonably do. How often do you think 'I couldn't do that?' As we grow up, the boundaries of what we think we can do get smaller. We literally learn, helped by the System's pressure, to cramp our own style. In spreading our Free Child wings, we might get the attention of other people. However, at this stage, gaining attention is not the primary aim. The time will come later to do this. Insofar as you do get the attention of others, you take their attention in turn away from the game they are playing, if only for a moment. To play our part in creating a movement, we need to gain attention from other people. Letting other people know what we're doing also gets attention, and gives the possibility of other people doing something themselves. We encourage others to express themselves if we do the same. Viral fashions, as we have seen, spread in this way – the selfie photos and the ice-bucket challenge are just two examples. It's important to tell your friends and colleagues what you're up to – that way, the approach might catch on.

With step one, we are learning to flex our Free Child muscles. We are getting used again to trying things out. While the actions in this step may seem trivial in themselves, we are subtly loosening the control society has over us, by starting to jettison the responsibility that has been foisted on us by the System game. We have started becoming a bit non-conformist in our own chosen ways, to test our boundaries to see what happens. We should play around with the authorities, just to see what happens. The authorities will struggle to cope with even this level of playful non-conformity!

This is a critical foundation for the next steps to playing a different game. Try it a few times just to see how it feels to throw off the shackles. Then you will be ready for the second game changer. This one involves taking responsibility for what you think, and expressing it. In other words we go to the second ego state in transactional analysis that is discouraged in the System game, that of Adult. Despite our society being largely rational on the surface, that does not mean that Adult behaviour is dominant, or even all that apparent.

Chapter 10 - Be real: Say what you stand for

- *Our lives begin to end the day we become silent about things that matter* – ***Martin Luther King Jnr.***

The second stage of moving towards a different game is to learn to be real again, and say what you stand for, and think. This is the phase of re-connecting with your Adult ego state, also not one that's encouraged by our society. We live in a society that says it encourages thought. However, it doesn't give space for real thinking. The pace of life has become so quick, with more and more activities being crammed into less and less time that we have no time to think. Never have we had access so many 'facts', and never have the tidal waves of facts we are engulfed with given us so little real knowledge or insight.

The 2014 Scottish referendum was a great example of this. Both sides in the referendum produced thousands of facts, pieces of research and viewpoints. What's more, all this information flatly contradicted the information provided by the other side. Anyone genuinely trying to make sense of it all would have self-destructed trying to process all this information, so they could decide which way to vote. Even as late as 10 days before the vote in a referendum that had lasted for the best part of two years, there were significant numbers of voters who weren't able to get their heads around both the scale of the decision facing them, and the volume of information they were expected to process.

What we do have is time to rationalise things. When we rationalise, we usually decide what to do, and then find some reasons that support our decision. Usually, we decide to do something conventional or low risk, and then rationalise why that is the best thing to do. Rationalising is the result of a combination of the dominant ego states in our System. We do the conventional thing, and often justify it by in some way putting the blame on other people, diplomatically or blatantly!

Rationalising things is not the same as thinking. Thinking is a good way to get yourself out of a hole, if you're in a hole to start with. Rationalising usually ends up justifying why you're in the hole in the first place! Thinking encourages you to move, rationalising encourages you to stay put by explaining why you should do so. Thinking is present and future focused, rationalising is about the past. Thinking leads to decision and action. Rationalisation leads to neither.

If there's one word that is used to describe the world we live in, that word is 'rational.' Rationality is a highly prized commodity, particularly in the Western world. We are generally expected to behave rationally. When I did my economics degree, all talk was of the rational consumer, buyer or seller. At work, rationality tends to be rewarded as a behaviour, and people who make decisions on more emotional grounds are often derided as 'weak.'

So what would Aristotle think?

Thinking has not always been as out of fashion as it is in the modern era. For example, if we go back to ancient Greece or Rome, thinking was all the rage. But then we had a profession that reflected that fact. It has often been said that the oldest profession in the world is prostitution. That may be, but the second oldest profession must surely be philosophy. Walk into a decent sized bookshop and you will find a range of timeless books by great philosophers like Aristotle, Plato, Socrates, and Seneca. If you want more up to date philosophy, you can try Locke, Machiavelli, Rousseau, Burke or Mill. If you want to be revolutionary, you can read the many works of Karl Marx. But then try becoming more modern than that, and you struggle to find any philosophical thinking whatsoever. Prostitution may be alive and well (if not healthy) in the modern era, but philosophy seems to have all but died out. With it, much of the accompanying thinking about life and society has died with it.

These philosophers all prized the role of thinking. Behind ancient philosophy was the idea that thinking was the way we could move forward as a species. The attainment of wisdom depended critically on thinking, and on thinking critically.

As modern life has rolled on, the death of philosophy was succeeded by the birth of something else, which now adorns the bookshelves of those same bookshops I've just spoken of. An entire industry has mushroomed, dedicated to promoting the well-being of the human race. That profession is self-help.

CREATE YOUR OWN REVOLUTION

Now I might be about to shoot my own messenger, given that I work in personal development and have written self-help articles and a couple of books in the past. However, here goes; self-help is not a good substitute for philosophy, even if some of the aims are the same. Both self-help and philosophy would concern themselves with how to build a happy life, so there is some common ground. However, there are some significant differences between them.

For one thing, philosophy often focused on the community as a whole, how to be happy in the context of a better society. Self-help applies the happiness aim to just me. Society is barely considered, unless doing something to help society is the thing that makes us happy. Self-help is all about me – how to lose weight, be healthy, eat well, become psychologically better, get my dream job, and so on. That is a huge shift, and represents nothing short of the privatisation of philosophy.

The other key difference is that much modern self-help comprises little more than platitudes that don't carry much thought behind them at all. Carried to its extreme, as exemplified in the best-selling self-help book *The Secret* you don't even need to do anything to get what you want. (1) You just have to wish for it with enough focus, and the universe will make it yours. Wishing is enough. You don't even have to think about what you want in any depth. How good is that? Come to think of it, how delusional is that? There's nothing wrong with being positive, and believing you can achieve things, but this approach takes it to an extreme. It is a self-perpetuating delusion because, if you fail to achieve what you're hoping for, it's only because you didn't wish for it hard enough. You allowed your head to talk yourself out of it. The Secret, and other books of its kind, don't encourage thinking to take place. If they did, you might work out that it has its limitations as a plan for action, and that would never do.

We've seen the move to shorter and shorter self-help books because people don't have enough time to read long ones. We've seen the growth of celebrity self-help, with more serious self-help books not being commercially published. Indeed, authors are often only published now if they can show that they're already well-known. We've been conditioned out of reading, as we have been conditioned out of thinking. We can see this through the declining attention spans of children. People increasingly skim information. We used to read letters, now we glance through an email. In the same way, we are discouraged from thinking, or from finding the time to do so. The most often used button on a PC while online is the back button. We read the first sentence on a website, and then decide to surf back out of it.

The trend in self-help has been to focus on the importance of our feelings, noticing what they are, and acting on them. This is clearly important. It is important to connect with our emotions if we want to find ways to improve our lives. Emotion gives life much of its meaning, and most of us want to feel in some way 'good.' However, the trend in self-help has gone well beyond this. The mantra has become a bit like 'feelings are good, thinking is bad.' However, this is to throw a very healthy baby out with some admittedly dodgy bathwater.

The conclusion is obvious. We need to seriously sharpen up on our thinking if we are to develop our potential and live the kind of life we want. Rationalising, by contrast, we can do without.

The irony is that what our society needs more than anything else is an outbreak of philosophy. We need to start thinking for ourselves again, and not let other people do our thinking for us. Modern self-help encourages us to connect with our emotions more, and there is nothing bad about this. But it is doing a disservice to our thinking, because we have become disconnected from that too. Don't feel too much, don't think too much, has become the way to cope with our society and its demands. But this is no way to a happy, fulfilling, genuinely productive life.

In other words, we need to feel like a Saint less, and perhaps think like the devil more!

Five reasons why we should think like the devil

I was brought up in a 'thinking' family. In childhood, I remember my mum saying to me on a number of occasions 'always think for yourself.' She meant that I should do my own thinking, and make my own mind up, not let others do this for me. Meanwhile, my father was the king of devil's advocacy, and he enjoyed nothing better than a good sparring match. I suspect he argued for the sake of it at times. No surprise then that I have developed a devil's advocate of my own. When it suits me, I can argue that black is white, even if I don't believe it myself!

So here are five reasons why thinking matters, or should matter.

1. It combats the black-white tendency

We live in a society that sees everything in terms of black and white, good and bad, okay and not okay, healthy and unhealthy. For example, we see sweeping generalisations being made about salt being bad for us. The trouble with this approach is that life is not black and white. Most people who have had to deal with problems know this to be true. Even the comment about salt is untrue. We would not survive if we had no salt in our body, so clearly at least some salt is good for us.

Thinking is healthy in enabling us to move away from a world of black and white.

2. Real thinking suspends judgement

We live our lives surrounded by judgements. From family, friends, bosses, colleagues, politicians, and everyone we interact with. Just think of the following words, and see what comes to mind – bankers, travellers, youths, and journalists.

Thinking about issues is one way to suspend judgement, not least because we spend some time working out our own conclusions from what we know. We make our own mind up. That's why Courts look at evidence before deciding.

Key to this is not confusing thinking with rationality - they are not necessarily the same thing. Thinking is coming to a conclusion or decision by examining the situation. Rationality often is reaching a conclusion, and then simply finding the facts to support the story!

3. We can control our thinking

Most of our brain operates at an unconscious or subconscious level, which means that in day to day life, we're not aware of what it does, and we are limited in what we can do to alter its operation. Unless that is, we get a therapist or psychiatrist.

Our conscious brain is the day-to-day engine that we can use, and thinking is the lubrication that makes that engine run. The quality of our life will depend greatly on how well we do this.

4. Thinking affects our emotions

What we think about affects how we feel. This is obvious, but it's amazing how often we can ignore the obvious. If we focus on uplifting things, our emotional state will improve. There is much evidence that how we think, and what we choose to focus on, affects both our mental and physical well-being.

5. Thinking is the key to progress

Thinking is key to both individual and collective progress in the human race. To take a cross section of people who are widely admired, what were Einstein, Gandhi, Martin Luther King, Nelson Mandela, Aristotle, Winston Churchill and Franklin Roosevelt if they weren't thinkers? So there you have it. Five reasons why thinking matters.

*****

The first step then to 'saying what you stand for' is to decide what you stand for, and this might take some thought. What actually matters to you? What's important? What would you change? Without delving too far into the realms of self-help, we need to become more self-aware – particularly of our values. If you've ever had that 'square peg in a round hole' feeling, it probably means that your own personal values are out of line with whatever it is you are doing, or being asked to do. It's stating the obvious to say for example that if I work in an investment bank, and one of my most important values is 'community' then there might be a tension between what I do and how I feel.

In saying this, I'm not advocating a touchy feely connection to emotion or values for its own sake. I am suggesting that to become better acquainted with how we feel is an important step to building our own self-awareness, and this will allow our Adult ego state to kick in with better information. We are then able to make better choices on what to do, and what to say.

The second step is to get your thinking hat on. We go along with what other people say far too often for our own good. But what do you actually think about things? This is particularly important for things that are important to you. Once you've done this, the next step is to begin articulating what you think. In other words, start talking to other people through whatever route you see fit - at work, in the pub, on Facebook, the phone, public meetings, over family meals, wherever you can find. There are a number of reasons why we should articulate our thinking, once we have done it.

To get support from others

One thing that stops us sometimes from talking about what matters to us is that it's 'just me.' We imagine that no-one else shares our concern or viewpoint. Talking about it is a great way to discover that other people have the same or similar thoughts to you. It is a great relief to find this out!

To refine your thoughts

We should think for ourselves. But that is not the same as shutting out other people's views. By listening to other people, we can sharpen our own thoughts. We might find a great way to express ourselves, or a new idea to integrate into our thinking. We learn from other people, and this can only improve our argument. Greek philosophers didn't just enjoy expressing themselves. They enjoyed the whole notion of philosophical debate and discussion. That is how they sharpened their arguments and refined their thinking. There's a difference between refining what you think, and giving up on it!

To influence others

Of course, if we can sharpen our thinking by talking with other people, then we're at the same time sharpening their thinking. In other words, we are influencing them. We cannot change anything in this society of ours unless we influence other people to start changing some aspect of what they do – and that begins with what they think.

To start mobilising opinion

By having some discussion and debate, we start in our own way to mobilise opinion. While we haven't all yet agreed to do anything as such, we start to become aware that we are far from alone in much of our thinking. What's more, if we are combining this step with the previous one, then we are doing naughty irrational things at the same time as talking to other people about what we think and why. We are but a short step away from creating a movement of people for change, and that is one of our key aims given what we know about society and the System we live under.

Saying what you stand for

One important thing is to say what you stand for, not just what you stand against. It's too easy in modern life to just be against everything. That's called cynicism! It might be understandable to some extent, but it won't improve anything. Nor does it make us feel better about anything. Simply being against things is no step forward. In Transactional Analysis terms, it means we are becoming either Parent or Adapted Child. All that means is that we are playing society's game, and not moving away from it. We need to learn to say what it is we are for.

I can give a personal example to illustrate this. In 2003, I was strongly opposed to the US and UK invading Iraq. I marched against the war, the first time in decades that I'd marched about anything. I wrote letters to newspapers on the subject, getting many of them published. I argued with my friends on the subject. I put a lot of energy into 'fighting' the decision to invade. But was I successful? The short answer is 'no.' I don't think I managed to change anyone's opinion. Perhaps the most significant reason why I failed was that I failed to express what I was for. I simply focused on what I was against. I behaved in a very Critical Parent / Adapted Child way. In short, I was one of the rebels that our System likes to have – it gives them someone to fight against. As usual when we rebel, we usually lose. This defeat was cemented by the national Groupthink phenomenon I mentioned in chapter three, when UK public opinion swung behind the war as soon as the bombing started.

It was Elvis Presley who, in 1960, was asked why he didn't resist US army conscription and so ended up serving abroad, while at the height of his rock and roll career. He replied that there was no use resisting the call because "they've never lost one yet!" Elvis recognised that rebelling against authority was futile, particularly because in this case, the authority was the US armed forces. Rebelling is futile, and one reason why it is lies in the point that we are fighting against something, not setting out what we are in favour of.

Talking big

Learning to talk bigger than we are is a key step in this process. What do I mean by this? It's easy to fall into one of the following traps when deciding whether or not to speak up on a particular subject.

- "I'm not as well qualified as those people over there."
- "I don't know enough about this to express an opinion."
- "He / she is in a powerful position, more powerful than me!"
- "I have no right to express an opinion on this."

Our society operates with a very powerful cult of expertise. We have experts in all walks of life who "know more than we do." They tell us how to live, how to feed our kids and where to invest our money. They tell us what a foreign government is up to and how best to deal with it. We see experts in all walks of life, on TV, in magazines, all advising us on what to do and think. Where does this come from? Why, it's our old friends 'Critical and Nurturing Parent' kicking in again! Of course, what they are looking for in response from the rest of us is a case of Adapted Child. Avoiding this trap will allow us to talk big. This means remaining in our Adult ego state in the first place.

We have all the brain we need to form a view, think it through, and express it in our own unique way. You do not need someone else to do this for you. It means connecting with your Adult, and being prepared to express views on wider issues, issues that are beyond your power to fix alone. But just because they are beyond your power doesn't mean you have no right to say what you think.

Say and be in tandem

Returning to the Gandhi principle, one trap to avoid is the one where we say one thing, and do another. The charge of hypocrisy is not one we want to be levelled at us.

One example I came across a few years ago was a hotel area manager in a holiday company, who spent much of his time bemoaning how 'political' the organisation was. He thought everyone was out to look after themselves, rather than do their best for the organisation. It was only after I spoke with other people in that organisation that I realised this manager was one of the most political people in the place. Needless to say, he was not seen by me as a very credible manager after this. His view on organisational politics certainly was not credible.

As mentioned before, it is important that we role model the changes we say we want. If you want society to be more democratic and consultative, then spending your time ordering your family around and not consulting with them is not going to strengthen the chances of your views being taken up! We won't be taken seriously, in the same way that more public figures are not taken seriously when they have that credibility gap between what they say and what they do.

For an example of the latter, take Alex Salmond and the 'Yes Campaign' in the Scottish referendum. I use this example to illustrate a point, not to take sides in the referendum. On the one hand, there was much talk about an 'inclusive' society, in which all people would be encouraged to make their contribution in an independent Scotland. On the other hand, we saw behaviour during the campaign, from the 'Yes Scotland' leadership that did not fit with this vision. We saw opponents derided for not being nationalistic enough – they are either with 'Team Scotland' or they are not. We saw advertising boards for the no campaign systematically ripped down and vandalised. We saw opponents of independence hounded and shouted down during public meetings and debates (although both sides were partially culpable of this.) Such behaviour simply doesn't sit easily with the 'inclusive' vision of Scotland that was portrayed.

On the other hand, let's consider a role model for this idea of 'saying and being.' A year or two ago, I saw a video, shot in India, depicting a traffic jam caused by a tree blocking a road. To make matters worse, it was muddy, and there were monsoon conditions. People sat in their cars and stood around, feeling frustrated and helpless. Then, a boy, who couldn't have been older than ten, started trying to push the tree off the road. A futile gesture, if ever there was one. Then a few other children joined him, out of camaraderie - and laughing as they pushed. After a while, some adults started to realise what they were trying to do, and joined in. Eventually, many others joined the push, and the tree was lifted, and moved off the road.

The message is clear. If that little boy had simply suggested to the adults that they push the car, he probably would have had no response. But by showing that he was prepared to modify his behaviour, and try to do it himself, he attracted hundreds of others to help. Being the change you want to see really does work!

Why this step matters

Saying what it is you stand for matters because it is about finding your cause, finding your voice, and finding your range. You are working out what you believe, expressing it, and connecting with other people. It is about connecting more effectively with both yourself and with other people. In taking this step, you are focusing your attention on what matters to you, and engaging with other people on it. You are also beginning the process of showing other people an alternative way of being. By learning to think and express yourself clearly, you will encourage others to do the same. By making sure that your conduct and behaviour matches up to your words, you will also be setting an example that will attract like-minded people to you. As we have already seen, people are often great copiers, and if they like what you're doing, they will copy you - and not just by imitating you. They will initiate their own thinking on what matters to them, and develop their own way to express their views.

By this stage, we have a group of people who are testing the boundaries, thinking differently, and talking about it. We will also have a better idea of our potential strength. But what do we do with this strength? How does this spark change in our society? How do we influence the System to shift? The third step I will talk about in the next chapter, shows exactly how we can do this.

Rediscovering our natural Adult means being prepared to gather our own thoughts and say them. It means not being afraid to talk about things that really matter to us. Finding your true voice, and connecting with other people on this, will raise the level of debate in our society beyond the current trivial, banal level. It is vital that, in doing this, we all practice what we preach. As Gandhi said many years ago, we have to be the change we want to see in the world. By this stage, the non-converted public will see significant numbers of people not only talking differently, but behaving differently. What's more, they will probably like what they see, and want to join the party.

Chapter 11 - Show your power

- *Do or do not. There is no try – **Yoda***

In the first of our three steps to revolution, we learned to play, to be disobedient, and test the boundaries the way we did as a child. We connected better with our Free Child ego state. In the second step, we began articulating our thoughts and views, and behaving in accordance with them. We connected better with our Adult ego state.

In carrying out these two steps, we have effectively administered an antidote to ourselves for the way society treats us. We have strengthened the very ego states that our dominant social culture doesn't encourage. We are now effectively starting to play a different game.

Now what? Here's what - the third step.

Showing your power means bringing together your Parent, Adult and Free Child - particularly the latter two. If we do too much Parent stuff, then we will risk reverting to the game society plays so well - of judging other people, giving disapproval, and treating other people as if they are stupid. People who come across as patronising are usually like this because they rely too much on the Parent ego state. Besides, Parent is usually about what other people 'should' do. As we have seen so far, the focus of this book is on what we should do for ourselves if we want things to be better in future.

What does 'show your power' mean then? It means engaging the System much more on our terms, not its terms. It would involve any or all of the following things:

- Conducting campaigns, or taking part in them, on anything from what's happening to your local school to national government policy.
- Campaigning to change the behaviour of business, where for example unethical practices are taking place - giving them bad publicity, taking our custom away, refusing to pay bills for a period of time, and so on.

- Positive civil disobedience. This might include non-voting, like spoiling your ballot paper, and other constructive forms of protest.

This stage means taking the small actions of stage one onto a different level. There are a number of key differences to the actions that take place at stage three. Firstly, there is more of a group or collective campaign, rather than the single act, which is more likely at stage one. Secondly, there is a more obvious desire to see something change as a result of these protests or actions. While we might still be testing the boundaries in that stage one way, we are more co-ordinated in wanting to bring about change. It is less about doing something for the sheer hell of it. Translating this into TA-speak, we are continuing with the Free Child's "what the hell" attitude, but applying it in an Adult way. We are taking responsibility for our actions, the results, and the possible outcomes.

To highlight how this might work, I'm going to illustrate with a few fictitious examples (though not all that fictitious!) Please note these are just examples, and not an exhaustive list. There are many things we could choose to campaign for, or indeed against.

- Google and Facebook's invasion of personal privacy on the internet. We could have a day of coordinated "let's post nothing on Facebook," or not use Google at all.
- We could campaign for improved public transport by going to our nearest motorway and sitting down to a picnic on it. How cool could that be? How many people would it take to close a motorway completely? A few thousand? Maybe even a few hundred?
- We could campaign in favour of improved banking practices (it would not be difficult to improve them!) by writing in significant numbers to give notice to close bank accounts, or just withdraw most of our money.
- We could protest against utility company price rises by not using energy for a day. Alternatively, we could all switch our kettles on at the same time, and bring the system down – for a little while at least. Emergency services have their own back-up power supplies, so they would not be affected.
- We could protest about the futility of party politics and the conduct of politicians by having a coordinated non-voting campaign. By turning out at election time and spoiling our ballot papers, we could make an active point, rather than sitting passively at home. Just what would happen if the spoilt ballot paper vote was higher than the winning

candidates vote? That would say much about the legitimacy of the political system, or lack of it.

These actions would not be comfortable to take – that's why building our muscles up through steps one and two would be so important. However, apart from eating our lunch on the motorway, most of these actions are entirely legal ones. That would make it difficult for the authorities representing the System to do anything about them, apart from criticise our irresponsibility that is! The irony of this is that responsibility for the future is precisely what we would be taking.

There are three important principles to bear in mind, if we are to become more of a collective movement and spark change within the System.

1. We must engage the System on our terms

It is vital that we don't get dragged into the System game, which is an easy trap to fall into. Importantly, this means that we need to stay positive. That means keeping our focus on what it is that we want to change or bring about. Even when acting against something we don't like, we need to try to avoid becoming negative in our tone. We can and should say what we are for, rather than what we're against.

To take the above example of Facebook compromising our privacy as users, it would be easy to settle for a protest slogan like "stop giving away our personal information to advertisers." While we might win a protest on these terms, we are unlikely to change things for the better in the longer term. A campaign slogan like "we want our right to privacy respected when we're online" is a better approach. It says what we're for, and avoids the temptation to become over-critical of other people. This approach keeps our Ego State in Adult mode, rather than lapsing into Critical Parent. We won't be able to change society by behaving in the same way as it does.

2. We do not need one leader

We're all responsible for leading any campaign we're involved in. This may sound strange or even absurd, but it's really important. We are all unique people with gifted talents, which we may or may not recognise for ourselves. Some people will inevitably make more noise than others, not least because they are naturally noisier, or used to 'being in charge' in life. However, it's important that we take responsibility for our own personal leadership, and not let others take charge. We also need to avoid trying to take charge ourselves. Imposing ourselves on other people won't change the System either.

There are two reasons why I believe taking our own personal leadership matters greatly.

First, if we move to having campaign leaders in the traditional sense, what are we doing when it comes to ego states? We are letting other people speak for us, or we are speaking on behalf of other people, depending on whether or not we're in the 'leadership'. In other words, we are moving towards a Parent - Adapted Child model of how to behave. We are choosing to comply with how our society wants us to behave! We're hardly playing a different game then, and we can expect the dominant System in our society to take advantage of this fact.

The second reason is that, by having leaders, we give the representatives of society someone to negotiate with, or otherwise try to influence. Our society loves to have that opportunity! Take street protests for example. Evidence shows that Police attempts to control protests usually centre on identifying the ring leaders, and then either negotiating with, or arresting, them. If it is the first tactic, the Police will negotiate in the hope that the leaders will then be able to influence their followers to go home. Where there are no protest leaders that can be identified, the Police attempts to control protests tend to break down spectacularly. They see no-one influential to negotiate with, or arrest.

In the same vein, Governments will usually try to negotiate with leaders of any movement to reach a settlement. If that fails, the next step is to diplomatically threaten them, or try to undermine them - ideally by provoking a change of leadership! In more authoritarian societies, leaders might also be arrested, or even killed. The aim of the System in every case will be to make the leadership more compliant, and then strengthen that leadership in hope that this encourages their followers to become more compliant in turn.

The lesson is clear. We need campaigns where everyone takes responsibility for their own leadership, rather than submitting to one or a few leaders. Try dealing with that, society!

The next principle is a logical implication of the one we've just talked about.

3. There is no one set of demands

We're not all going to agree on absolutely everything. Even if we think things through carefully (and many people don't do this!) we will still have differences of opinion. Great philosophical thinkers and debaters didn't reach 100% agreement, so we're not going to achieve this either. This means that we're not going to have one set of demands. We may have hundreds if not thousands of demands, many of which will be similar but not identical.

This is okay. In fact, it is good! But it is completely different from what we're used to. How would this work, and why is it good? Again, let's consider that question from the perspective of our dominant society approach. What do they want? What is it the System looks for?

If society's representatives face a challenge, the one thing they want ideally (apart from the challenge to go away) is a list of demands. That list then becomes a basis for negotiation, hopefully with potential for compromise. If there is a single leadership, then so much the better. With one set of demands, society can do one of two things - reject the demands and try and win the dispute, or compromise and settle so everyone goes home. Either way, society knows what it's dealing with, so it has one thing it wants - some degree of certainty.

That certainty is removed if there isn't one set of demands. We all have our own individually unique set of wants, but we are acting in collaboration with others who agree enough with us to work with us. The System is not set up to deal with this. If 5000 bank customers write to their bank in a coordinated campaign to give notice to quit, and publicise it wherever they can, the bank can't negotiate to reach a settlement. But it will have bad publicity and a drop in its share price to deal with, so it's going to have to change some aspect of its behaviour.

These then are the three key principles underpinning this stage of action. By adopting them, we are able to truly show our power as a movement of leaders. But let's remind ourselves just why we want to do this. What is the point of taking this approach?

The aim of this step

The aim of this step is to spark or provoke change in the System, and not to reach a settlement with it. One implication of this approach immediately becomes clear. There is no end point to this approach. This is not about reaching a compromise with the System, and settling for it. This step represents a change forever. It is at this point that, by changing our game, we start to change society's game. It has to change to adapt.

By not conforming to social norms on demands and leadership, we have effectively by-passed the System's normal ways of dealing with things it doesn't like. We also show the fragility of the System and the way it works to other people who may now decide to jump on board - especially when they realise this is the way to change things. While we may not be highlighting the System as having 'no clothes' on, in the words of that childhood tale, we are certainly highlighting it as having a rather deficient, out of date wardrobe! (1)

Once we have reached the stage of showing our power in this way, we are now in what would effectively be a different ongoing relationship with the System. There is no backing out, and no end to the process. That again is a good thing. If we want ongoing change, then we need a different ongoing relationship.

In summary

This stage brings the first two steps together in a focused campaign. This will be civil, and at times disobedient, in nature. Critically, it will also be publicised, and it will be down to all of us to publicise it ourselves and not rely on others to do so. An example would be 'positive non-voting,' where we spoil our ballot papers by writing on the back what we want to see, instead of simply not voting. If only 10% of the population did this, it would force our political leaders to start taking notice. As we have seen over decades of disappointment, elections change nothing of any significance. By this stage, we would be engaging with society on our terms. We would not have one set of 'demands,' nor would we have one leader. Instead, we would all be leading in our own true way. The aim of this sort of campaigning is to spark change within the System, not to reach a settlement with it, or to overthrow it. By in effect by-passing the system, we would spark an ongoing dialogue, and change in our society.

CREATE YOUR OWN REVOLUTION

We have now covered the three steps to revolution, sparking our society and the dominant System into change because it would have no alternative to doing so. Hopefully, this sounds simple, and I hope too that you buy the idea and approach.

However, you would not be human unless there were a few cautionary voices going off inside your head. These voices may be saying things like:

- I'm not good / important enough to do this!
- Society would clamp down on us, it wouldn't work.
- It will inevitably end up in disappointment.
- I might get burned if I take a few risks.
- Some people would inevitably end up leading this, and then it doesn't work anymore.
- How can I cooperate with people if they don't agree with me?

These are all understandable positions to take. In the final two chapters, we will look at how we move above these challenges to become part of the future development of our society, as well as living a better life for ourselves and those who matter to us. This matters, because we have an opportunity to change things like never before.

Part 3 - Being part of the future

Chapter 12 - Transcending our society

- *Twenty years from now you will be more disappointed by the things you didn't do than by the ones you did do. So throw off the bowlines. Sail away from the safe harbour. Catch the trade winds in your sails. Explore. Dream -* **Mark Twain**

We are born with very few limitations, or at least we're not aware of any. We believe we can fly, metaphorically and perhaps literally! Never mind, we'll soon get that illusion bashed out of us. Along with illusions about us being good, talented, worthy, and important. The only people who end up still believing they are these things on arrival at adulthood are very lucky. Even narcissistic people don't necessarily believe these things, which is why they keep looking at themselves for reassurance.

This education we receive in our formative years imbues us with a range of beliefs about ourselves, and other people, that get in our way. A far from exhaustive list of these beliefs would include the following. Do you recognise any of these as your own?

- I must always make sure I get permission.
- I must never make a mistake.
- I'm not a very interesting person.
- I must not show how I feel.
- Questioning authority is not acceptable.
- To say what I want is rude.
- I should be quiet unless spoken to.
- I must make sure I'm busy.

- I'm not worthy of being liked.
- I must not say no to anyone else.

Now, I'm not here to recommend how to deal with all of these largely negative or limiting beliefs. Instead, I'm going to invite you to consider that there may be two ways we can look at this issue of how we deal with our limitations. We can either try to overcome our limiting beliefs about ourselves and other people, or we can simply choose to transcend them.

When we try to overcome limiting beliefs, we are heading down the self-help or therapy - counselling road. It often involves finding out where each limiting belief came from in the first place, and then trying to modify or change it. This usually means talking about the past, which for many ends up being a painful experience. It is no surprise then that many people try to avoid doing this.

Most of these limiting beliefs are Adapted Child in nature, as we moved away from being all powerful new-born human beings. We have cramped our own style as parental figures in our childhood criticised us, or taught us lessons. These lessons are now basically voices inside our heads, and they are Critical Parent in nature. Yes, you've guessed it! Not only does the Critical Parent - Adapted Child axis rule in the System we live under, but it's also the System we live with inside our own heads. Given this fact, we can either play the game, or choose to play a different game. This game would be a more Free Child - Adult game, which might look more like 'bugger it, let's not worry about the past or the future, but just live in the present.' As the old saying goes, you get what you focus on. If you choose to focus on your own limitations, you get limitations. A life with limitations is in whose interest exactly? It certainly isn't in your interest!

So what is the alternative?

The alternative to this is to transcend our limiting beliefs, to simply choose to rise above them. By rising above them, we don't need to overcome them, or to bust through them. In this way, we adopt the Principle of Transcendence. This principle is an ironic one. It involves us in learning not to see our beliefs as 'the enemy.' Just imagine for a moment lacking self-confidence as the result of a belief about being 'no good.' If you see the belief as the enemy, you end up thinking "I wish I didn't have such a negative belief. Why am I not capable of thinking something more positive about myself?" Can you see where this is going? Yes, the next step is "I wish I was a less negative person!" Suddenly it's not the belief that's the enemy. Instead, we have become our own enemy. It's either that, or we end up blaming other people for our belief – "it's your fault I feel like this!" By seeing the belief and whatever lies behind it as our enemy, we end up going nowhere fast.

The Principle of Transcendence applies just as much to society. After all, if we end up seeing our beliefs as the enemy, we end up blaming ourselves or other people for this. It's a short step from here to blaming society, or certain sections of it, more generally. We start to blame other people for the ills in society, whatever we think they are. Again, how often have you heard statements like "if it wasn't for these 'do gooders', bankers, politicians, civil servants, Faceless bureaucrats, etc."

The beauty of the Principle of Transcendence when we look at the System of society is that we stop seeing certain groups of people as the enemy. We stop seeing society itself as the enemy. In a similar vein, we rise above it all. These groups of people I've just mentioned are just as much pawns of this play called the System as we are. They are pawns of the System, even if we don't like some of what they decide to do, say or be. By no longer seeing enemies, we become more Adult in our approach, and less susceptible to the Critical Parent or Adapted Child approaches so often promoted in our play of society. We no longer need to overcome our society or sections of it. We just need to play a different game, and that involves transcending things more often. It means not seeing enemies, either within or outside our own heads.

It means making a conscious choice to not blame ourselves, other people, or the System as a whole, for the things we see that are wrong. If we resort to blame, we are playing the game, and not transcending it.

Other magical things will start to happen if we adopt this principle in our lives. Here are just two of them.

Differences seem less different

When we no longer look for blame in others, we spend less time obsessing on what distinguishes us from other people. Differences don't matter to the same extent, whatever those differences happen to be. Whether nationality, personality styles, profession, upbringing, religious or cultural aspects, they matter less to us. After all, if we're not looking for someone to blame, why should differences matter that much? What happens instead is we start to notice what unites us, rather than what divides us. We realise how similar we all are, underneath the costumes we wear in this System generated show. That's why barriers between people often begin to break down when we start talking to each other.

Of course, our existing System won't like this one bit in practice, even if lip service is paid to the idea of tolerance. Divide and rule is the rule our society has evolved to follow, engendering fear, intolerance and blame. Society's attempts to retain our attention play to this game, with its emphases on crises, and the need for 'bad guys' to blame. With the Principle of Transcendence, we can choose not to play this game anymore. We can choose not to play no matter the tactics we face.

Like the spoilt child it is, the System would no doubt play a more extreme Critical Parent – Adapted Child game to convince us to get back on board, particularly when many of us detach from the game. It would look for ringleaders, and we might see its power used in a more obvious way. Could people be arrested and prosecuted for threatening to close their bank accounts in the hope of discouraging other people from doing this in future? Could the risk of collapse to our civilisation (I joke not!) be used to justify internment, or even more restrictions on our civil liberties than we face already? Could we even see spoiling our ballot papers turned into a criminal act?

The powers that be might try. But if we stick to the Principle of Transcendence and the three steps as outlined in preceding chapters, our focus would remain on the idea of playing a different game, rather than seeing those in society as the enemy. And this is the key to disengaging from the game, making society change in response. If enough of us can do this often enough, then we will see some real change take place.

Keeping our perspective

By adopting this principle, we will gain a much better sense of perspective on life, and what goes on within it.

After all, as the economist John Maynard Keynes once observed, "in the long run, we're all dead anyway." (1) What sort of society do you want your children to be part of once you're gone? Do you want them to be part of the society we're in currently, or would you like it to be better than that? Realising that in the long run we're all dead is a great way to keep perspective, and to notice how absurd the play that is society actually is. Show me someone in crisis and I'll show you someone who has lost perspective. Society relies on our losing perspective so it can tell us what our perspective ought to be. Then, like good little sheep, we can either buy the story or push back on it, and become a rebel. But, in choosing to see an enemy, we are ironically signing up to play a role in the game. Disengaging from the game and doing something more worthwhile instead is the only place to be.

The system's retort to transcendence

It's important to remember that, in transcending the game, we need to avoid being dragged back in to the System game, and to stick to our own.

Some of the principles of this game are all pervading. Just turn on a TV, listen to politicians and business leaders, and not a few psychologists and others. When you do so, you will hear the following points of view being expressed.

- We are all ultimately self-interested, and will put our needs ahead of other people. After all, it's a dog-eat-dog world out there.
- It's just human nature, and you can't change that. It's all about survival of the fittest.
- We have an innate need for order and stability. It is dangerous to put this at risk.

If we accept these arguments as the sum total of the truth, there's no real hope for any change. But the trouble is there's lots of evidence that human beings are not just like this. So let's consider a more rounded response to this caricatured evidence.

The riposte to the System

Yes, it is true that human beings are to some extent self-interested. But we are also interested in other people, and are social animals too. Just look at the way that huge sums of money have been raised for charitable causes, from Band Aid and Live Aid onwards. Many people, perhaps most, also want a greater cause to believe in, and simply making money does not fulfil that cause. Economies are meant to serve the needs of people, not the other way round. Otherwise, why have one? We have one because it represents the opportunity to advance our civilisation.

CREATE YOUR OWN REVOLUTION

Human nature can be brutal, but it can also evolve. After all, we don't all go around murdering people the way we would have done a few hundred years ago. We co-operate to a great extent, on many things. It's a shame that it often takes disaster to bring this to the surface. But take the Asian Tsunami in 2004, or the attacks on New York and Washington in 2001, or the London bus bombings in 2005, and we saw people go out of their way to help others in distress, often at great risk to themselves. That was not the action of self-interest. If we choose to believe the stuff we are fed by our old System leaders, then we ought to go back to murder and mayhem. So let's continue to evolve instead – it's time for the next step to be taken.

It is true that many revolutionary and reform movements have failed in the past, and we have looked at why this is so. The irony of the communist revolutions is that they overthrew the tyrants, but left the tyrannical machinery of state in place. So, once other people (now revolutionaries) entered the stage, they started to play the game as it was before. The only thing that changed was just who was in charge. At times this had terrifying results, as anyone who has studied Stalin's reign in the Soviet Union will tell you. Leadership, responsibility and power did not pass over to the people. They simply ended up being ruled by another source, the new pigs of Orwell's animal farm. (2)

Putting what happened to one side for a moment (not easy I know!), much of the communist critique of capitalism and its effects have been proved right. Global capitalism is destroying the planet, despite some attempts at reform. Businesses have become bigger, more global and all powerful, not to mention monopolistic. Real wages have declined in the USA and UK in the last forty years. The machinery of state essentially exists to serve the needs of big business, and Government is becoming more subservient by the minute. Even now, international laws are being campaigned for which would allow global businesses to sue Governments for damages if they take actions that cause business to lose money. Where will that leave old style democracy in the Western world, apart from dead? Karl Marx and other radical and revolutionary writers could have foreseen much of this. The communist critique was, and is, essentially correct in its diagnosis.

So where did they fail? Not for the reasons usually attributed by supporters of the current capitalist System. They didn't fail because they misread human nature, meaning that self-interest would rule no matter who was in charge. Nor did it fail because capitalist competition led to such great performance. Indeed, China puts that theory to the test, the way they have outgrown the West for most of the last thirty years. There are now more millionaires in Shanghai than New York.

Communism didn't fail because it misread human nature. Communism failed because, while Communists claimed to like 'the people' in their literature, most of their leaders didn't actually like people in real life! Lenin, Stalin, Trotsky and others didn't exactly go out of their way to engage with human beings. Harangue and preach to them perhaps. If that tactic didn't work, imprison and shoot them. If you don't like real people, you're hardly going to let them assume responsibility for their own lives.

The west might be more benign than this (though Afghanis, Iraqis and others may contest this point), but the power structures and assumptions remain similar. Let's return to Scotland, where the 'Yes' campaign leaders in the independence referendum simultaneously proclaimed their love for Scotland and the Scots while branding opponents as "not real Scots" and "not part of team Scotland". A classic them and us tactic. What's more, within 48 hours of the referendum result, they were actively considering ways to overturn the result of the people's vote by reneging on an undertaking made before the referendum, that this was a once in a generation opportunity. This is to my mind another example of liking the idea of the people in theory, but being contemptuous of them in real life – especially if they don't do what you want!

The message is clear. The people need to transcend this game and take their own power. What's more, any genuine change if it is to work must be based on the opposite principle to the above. It must be based on liking people in real life, and respecting their right to take their power – even if we don't agree with them. We don't have to agree. If we want a tolerant, just, fair and engaged society, then we must practice tolerance, being just, fairness and engaging with others in proper dialogue about things that matter – to us and to them. As Gandhi said, the means are the end.

Now that would be a true revolution!

In summary

To fulfil our role in changing things means being part of society, but being independent of it at the same time. We transcend our society – there is no need to 'overcome' it. We do not need to push the System over in some big rebellion. By taking our attention elsewhere and playing a different game, we remove the scaffolding the System relies on, which is the attention we give it. With less attention, the System will fall of its own accord, or it will learn to accommodate us.

We also transcend our own limiting beliefs about ourselves, the beliefs that provide us with hang ups. I call this the principle of transcendence. By doing this, we simultaneously transcend the divisions within, and between, societies. We emphasise what unites us rather than what divides us.

The existing power structures within our society will, of course, attempt to regain our attention as any spoilt child would do. It would seek out the ringleaders, to negotiate with, buy off, harass or arrest. Our media would emphasise crises, and no doubt a pretext would be found to fight a war somewhere. These are all tactics designed to regain our attention and induce fear. However, this would not work if we stick to the principles talked about in the last few chapters.

In the long run, we are all dead anyway, so keeping a sense of perspective is vital. Humour and play will help with this. What sort of society do you want your children to be part of? The one you're living in, or better than this?

The final step in our journey to transform society for the better lies in dealing with one of the last statements I made. With any organisation, society will try to find and isolate the ringleaders. So how do we make sure our organisation doesn't have any?

Chapter 13 – A movement, not an organisation

- *If your actions inspire others to dream more, learn more, do more and become more, you are a leader* - ***John Quincy Adams, 1767-1848***

It is my intention to create a picture of hope, an approach to sparking change for the better in our sick society. However, there remains one large concern, which underpins most of the past failures to change our society. Many movements with their demands for change in society have ultimately fallen short of their target, and been incorporated into society's dominant game. In some cases, like the British Labour Party or equal opportunities movements, some goals were achieved. But, in most cases, the game changed little, as the sight of UK West Indians complaining about the influx of Rumanians illustrates. The actors and actresses have changed, but the game of divide and rule remains the same.

What is it that happened to these organisations? The answer to the question is that they were organisations in the first place. They were traditional western style organisations, with sets of often centrally agreed (or imposed) rules, and a leadership structure that was imposed or agreed to. Having leaders in an organisation is like having handles on a pot – it makes it all the easier for the System to grab a hold of it. What's more, that is usually what the System does. Its tactics for doing this vary, but the main principles are as follows – and not in any order.

Ring fence the organisation
The System's aim here is to identify who is, and is not, a member of the organisation. The System attempts to define the contents of the pot. Achieving this is the first step towards containment, and once the members are known, there are many things that can happen. If we are talking about a demonstration, the System will literally ring fence the demonstrators.

Identify its demands
The System will try to identify what it is the members of this organisation actually want. This enables a decision to be made on the likelihood of being able to reach a compromise if necessary. This step is made easier if the next step can also be taken.

CREATE YOUR OWN REVOLUTION

Identify its leaders
The System will look out for the leaders. Who they are, what they're like, and what they want. If there appear to be no leaders, the System looks for them, encouraging them to emerge – for example, by talking to a delegation representing the organisation. The hope is that this delegation will eventually become the leadership.

Identify how it works
Now that it knows the demands and the leadership, the System can better grab hold of the pot. However, it will also want to gauge how the organisation works. What are the ground rules the organisation works by?

Reach a conclusion
Now the System is ready to make its move, though it can take a considerable period of time to reach the conclusion. The Systems leaders (political or business) will negotiate with the leadership on the demands of the organisation. It will aim to reach some sort of compromise if it cannot successfully reject the demands being made. If the organisation's leaders reject a compromise, the System will change tack, and find ways to isolate and undermine the leaders, or even to reject and fight the organisation.

The System aim in all this is always the same; to assimilate the organisation and its leadership. To integrate the organisation back into the System's own game. Once this is achieved, we're back at the start!

Given this picture, what do we do to spark sustainable long term change that doesn't end up like the above scenario? Basically, we need to break the above cycle, so society cannot 'get a handle' on us. Here are my thoughts on how we might do it.

1. Forget the organisation, create a movement!

The first place to break the cycle is to create a movement, and not to bother with the organisation. We do not need a well-organised, well drilled machine to lobby for change. In fact, it is the last thing we need. How can the power brokers grapple with an organisation if there isn't one? They simply cannot do it! We do not need chairpersons, secretaries, organisers, treasurers or anyone else with a formal title. We simply need a movement of people who hold common ground on what needs to change in the society we live in.

CREATE YOUR OWN REVOLUTION

One of the points to playing a different game is to recognise that we are all valid, and have a contribution to make. Our old game society doesn't recognise this fact. We need a movement of engaged individuals who come together because we can see there has to be a better way to be – that things can be much, much better than they currently are. This is the energy that will spark change in society.

The irony of the Scottish independence referendum is that it did lead to a historically high level of engagement in political terms. People divorced from politics for decades got themselves interested in the debate about the future of Scotland. This latent energy exists across the whole of western society, just waiting for a cause to spark it. The top-down nature of the independence movement would not have generated the change, ironically, as the Scottish Government leadership does not stand to fundamentally change the game being played. Besides, the Scottish economy is wired into the UK and Western economies. Governments won't change this game, because they have too much to lose. But people can do this – next steps please!

If we look at Carne Ross's take on the Occupy Wall Street movement, it started out as this type of movement. Initially in Zuccotti Park in New York, the initial demonstration began a global protest movement aimed at Wall Street, and the financial capitalist system. (1) What made this a different type of movement, at least initially, was the emphasis on ordinary people speaking up, and being listened to. Ross goes on to point out that human beings aren't the purely self-serving, self-interested creatures our dominant culture assumes they are. Instead, they also "value other qualities - compassion, meaning, community, beauty". The movement was also characterised initially as one where people genuinely listened to each other in a way that was far more empathetic than anything our society's leaders manage to do.

Other movements that are emerging also seem to reflect this emphasis on a more spontaneous action being taken, rather than relying on an organisation with a centralised leadership. The online movement 'SumOfUs' is another example. (2) On its website, the movement is described as a "movement of consumers, workers and shareholders speaking with one voice to counterbalance the growing power of large corporations. Join us on our journey as we seek to make the world a better place for ourselves, our children and all who share our planet."

So far, SumOfUs has sparked significant numbers of fundraising and petition movements aimed at taking on big corporations who are engaged in what are seen as unethical (even if legal) practices. We will see whether this movement manages to remain one, or whether it evolves into a more conventional organisation.

2. Forget the list of demands

If the System needs a defined organisation to grapple with successfully, it also needs a set of demands to be made. The implication of this is clear and ironic; if we want to be successful in changing our society, we need to forget about that list of demands! By having no one set of demands, there is nothing to compromise on. Instead, what we have is a movement where each of us has our own demands, where we keep in touch with each other, and coordinate some of our actions using social media and other channels. What's more, our individual demands will not be the same! The things that frustrate, upset, dispirit and annoy each of us are not the same things, even if we agree on the point that society is sick and in need of overhaul.

All we need to do is to keep in contact with others and take action where we need to. Our society will have to adapt to those demands if enough people act in support of what we want to see. All we need to do is avoid letting other people tell us what our own demands are.

This is not to say that, if we genuinely talk to others that we won't find a lot of common ground with other people. We might find that we end up agreeing in principle on 70-80% of the issues that are out there. The point is that we don't turn this 70-80% agreement into a list of demands. That would be playing into the hands of the System.

3. We are all leaders!

If we are a movement not an organisation, and we have thousands if not millions of individual sets of demands, then one point follows inextricably from this. We become a movement of leaders rather than a movement with leaders. In other words, there is no one leader or group of leaders. Instead, we are all leaders!

Yet again, this will frustrate the traditional leaders in our society, who will want a group of leaders who have authority to talk on behalf of their followers. Leaders are another lever that the System won't hesitate to use in an attempt to regain control. So if we have none, there can be no control in the traditional sense of the word. To be more accurate, we would all be leading in our own way. No doubt some people would be more vociferous than others, but that doesn't mean we should automatically follow them. That would not be playing a different game, it would be playing the same game.

Society has a simple rule of thumb when it comes to organisations and leaders. The best outcome is to have a pliable leadership that can be manipulated by the System, and who have enough formal power to make their followers fall into line with whatever is agreed. The second best outcome for society if this is not attainable is militant leadership. While negotiations might prove difficult, at least the System knows who it has to deal with. History tells us that our 'old game' leaders will talk to whoever is in charge, no matter who they are, or how repugnant they may be. Terrorist leaders, leaders of nasty regimes and corrupt business leaders have all found their way into the corridors of power by virtue of their being leaders in the first place.

The worst case scenario for our 'old game' leaders is an organisation with no leadership, or at least no identifiable group of leaders. They then have no one to negotiate with, no one to threaten, and no one to buy off. There is no deal on the table. A co-operative movement where everyone leads is our best chance of making the 'old game' change. It would have to change because it would no longer work.

As with riots and large demonstrations, society behaves as the police behave. They look for leaders to control, and if they can't find any, they know they are in trouble!

We are all part of the debate and part of the solution to the old game. It is not down to someone else to solve the problem. It is down to each of us to play our part by showing whatever leadership we are able to. This point has been strongly made by the advocates of the Occupy Wall Street movement. However, it is not 'leaderless change' as they suggest. It is the opposite of that! It is a 'leaderful change' with everyone adopting their own unique leadership role, on the things and in the ways that most matter to them.

4. No negotiation, and no fighting!

It follows from all I have said, that there is no negotiation to be had with authority, on behalf of the movement. We will each have our own individual negotiations depending on what it is we are doing, who with and why we are doing it. Groups of people might negotiate, but that would not tie in the rest of the movement, who might have nothing to do with what you're doing. Indeed, the rest of the movement might not even agree with your demands!

In addition to this, it's important to keep remembering that we are not 'fighting' anyone. We are all collectively victims of this old game, even those who still act in accordance with its rules. They are probably no happier than we are, they just haven't worked it out yet, or cling to the idea that things cannot get any better. We are not out to fight their game, or to win. We are out to play a different game, and in so doing, to help other people realise that they would be better off to change their game as well.

Take a walk on the wild side

I am inviting you to take a walk on the wild side. Most research says that people are more likely to go to the grave regretting what they didn't do in their lives, than go to the grave regretting what they did do. There is no wilder place to walk than on the event horizon.

What is an event horizon? For those of you who don't know, it is a phenomenon found next to a black hole, in space. Inside a black hole, which is a collapsed star, nothing can get out. Not even light. Outside the black hole, matter and light are free to move around according to their laws. The borderline between the two is called the event horizon – matter and light orbiting the border, not falling into the black hole, and not breaking away from it either.

Right, that's the astronomy lesson over! Now it's time to think of yourself as an individual event horizon, because if we are to spark change in our society, that is what we need to be. We need to walk the borderline between our existing society, and the vision we have about our 'different game' and what could be excitingly different about our society. If we simply cut ourselves off from society, and go into our own version of 'outer space' we lose the chance to influence other people. On the other hand, if we allow ourselves to get dragged back into society's game, to get caught up in the drama of crisis, blame and frantic activity for the sake of it, then we perform the equivalent of falling back into the black hole. We need to remain on the borderline, the event horizon. That way, we stay in a relationship with society without getting stuck in it. Keeping in with our Free Child and Adult ego-states is the key combination to achieve this, the very combination our 'old game' doesn't want.

So feel free to opt in and opt out of society. That's a better option than disengaging completely from it and walking away. But always remember that when you engage with society, you will be subject to the pressures it exerts to play the old game. Being in society, but not of society, is the trick we must pull off. Finding ways to articulate the new game and taking action will help to counteract this pull towards mediocrity.

Engaging with the community, and disengaging from the game, is the key to transformational change in our society. With our increased awareness of what's going on, and its impact on us if we're not careful, we have the opportunity to do something different and exciting. Self-awareness plus selective disengagement is the challenge we must rise to.

In summary

Creating our movement means that we reach a different relationship with the society we are all part of. This relationship involves disengaging from the game, articulating what we want, and making change happen. But this doesn't happen in the way it has in the past. Instead, we create a movement for change, not an organisation. There is no organisation in the traditional sense, with leaders who speak 'on behalf' of everyone else. No-one has the right to speak for you. Instead, this is a movement of leaders.

The beauty of this approach is that our society with its traditional structures won't be able to deal with such a movement. It will look for leaders and traditional structures to engage with. Unable to deal with this, our society will have to change, and power will shift with this. By making our unique contribution and engaging with our communities, friends and colleagues, we play our part in sparking change. We are all part of the debate, and the solution – it isn't down to 'someone else' to do it for us. We can, and must, do it together.

Postscript

- *It's not the size of the dog in the fight, it's the size of the fight in the dog* - **Mark Twain**

There we have it. As individual human beings, we have immense power to change things. By working with others, we have the power to transform the society we live in, moving away from the traditional Parent-Child system we have at the moment. We are all unique individuals, and have great potential to be whatever we want to be. Our society does not condition us to believe this, but it is true nonetheless.

By adopting the principles referred to in this book, we will be instrumental in changing the power structures in our society, and moving towards a much more Adult-Adult society, in which we will become much more than simply workers and consumers. Bringing out more creative approaches to life, speaking our own truth while respecting who we are, and connecting with our own power, will not only make our own lives better. It will improve the lives of others around us. Even those we see as gaining from the current System often only gain economically, at the expense of their own development as human beings. They are no happier than the rest of us. They are as much a prisoner of their part of the play as we are a prisoner of ours. It's time to play our break out of jail cards.

People of the world unite! You have nothing to lose but your brains. It's time to fix our broken society.

*****

References

Part 1 – The problem with society

Chapter 1 – What we all know

1. From www.trusseltrust.org
2. www.highpaycentre.org, 16th June 2014
3. www.theguardian.com, 22nd November 2011
4. Source: www.cipd.co.uk, 'UK's top bosses paid 143 times more than their average employee', by Grace Lewis. Deborah Hargreaves was quoted in this article.
5. Claire Crawford & Wenchao Jin, *Payback time?* Student debt and loan repayments: What will the 2012 reforms mean for graduates?, IFS Report R93, April 2014, P8
6. Source: BBC website, "Viewpoint: 10 big myths about World War One debunked", by Dan Snow

Chapter 2 – The 'Big society' game

1. George Orwell, 1984, Penguin, 2013. First published in 1949
2. Aldous Huxley, *Brave New World*, Vintage Classics, 2007. First published 1932
3. Claire Crawford & Wenchao Jin, *Payback time?* Student debt and loan repayments: What will the 2012 reforms mean for graduates?, IFS Report R93, April 2014, P20
4. Sir Ken Robinson, 'Do schools kill creativity?' TED talk (Technology, Entertainment, Design), 2006. This talk can be found either on www.ted.com, or on YouTube
5. Abraham Maslow, *Motivation and personality*, Harper New York, 1954
6. Richard D Wolff, Capitalism hits the fan: The Global Economic meltdown and what to do about it, Interlink Books, 2nd Revised edition, 2013.
7. Royal Charter for the Continuance of the British Broadcasting Corporation, Department for Culture, Media and Sport, October 2006
8. George Orwell, *1984*, Penguin 2013. First published in 1949
9. Sir Ken Robinson, *Changing Education Paradigms*, RSA Animate, October 2010. This talk can be found on www.thersa.org

10. www.fortune.com, 5 companies that pay CEO's big for a job poorly done, Chris Matthews, 17.6.14
11. www.theguardian.com, 6.11.12, Executive pay up 27% despite backlash, Juliette Jowit

Chapter 3 – Our connivance in this game
1. Reported in the *Guardian* newspaper, 24th September 2014
2. Irving Janis, *Victims of Groupthink*: a Psychological Study of Foreign-Policy Decisions and Fiascos, Boston: Houghton Mifflin 1972
3. Irving Janis, *Victims of Groupthink*: a Psychological Study of Foreign-Policy Decisions and Fiascos, Boston: Houghton Mifflin 1972, p9

Chapter 4 – Capitalism and democracy
1. The original idea of 'Doublethink' can be found in; George Orwell, *1984*, Penguin 2013. First published in 1949
2. Reported in the *Independent* newspaper, 21st February 2014, reporter Charlie Cooper
3. Reported on the BBC website news on 13th February 2014, www.bbc.co.uk

Chapter 5 – Analysing the game
1. For an in depth introduction to Transactional Analysis, see Ian Stewart and Vann Joines, *TA Today*: A New Introduction to Transactional Analysis, Lifespace Publishing, 2nd revised edition, 2012
2. Dr Eric Berne, *Games People Play*, Penguin, 2010

Chapter 6 – The System's weaknesses
None.

Part 2 – Creating the solution

Chapter 7 – Regaining our lost talents
1. Sir Ken Robinson, 'do schools kill creativity?' TED talk (Technology, Entertainment, Design), 2006

Chapter 8 – The opportunity to change
1. *Time Magazine*, July 7th 1967

2. First mentioned in; Joe Girard, *How to sell anything to anybody*, Simon & Schuster Ltd, 2006

Chapter 9 – Regain our playful, creative side
None.

Chapter 10 – Be real: Say what you stand for
1. Rhonda Byrne, *The Secret*, Atria, 2006

Chapter 11 – Show your power
1. Hans Christian Andersen, *The Emperor's New Clothes*, Houghton Mifflin Harcourt, 2014. First published 1837

Part 3 – Being part of the future

Chapter 12 – Transcending our society
1. J M Keynes, *A tract on monetary reform*, Lightning Source Incorporated, 2009. First published 1923
2. George Orwell, *Animal Farm*: A Fairy Story, Secker and Warburg, 1945

Chapter 13 – A movement, not an organisation
1. Carne Ross, *Occupy Wall Street* and a *New Politics for a Disorderly World*, Published in 'The Nation', February 7th 2012
2. Found at www.sumofus.org

Lightning Source UK Ltd.
Milton Keynes UK
UKOW06f1015110316

270017UK00007B/121/P